WordPress® in One Hour FOR LAWYERS

How to Create a Website for Your Law Firm

JENNIFER ELLIS

ABA LAW PRACTICE DIVISION
The Business of Practicing Law

Commitment to Quality: The Law Practice Division is committed to quality in our publications. Our authors are experienced practitioners in their fields. Prior to publication, the contents of all our books are rigorously reviewed by experts to ensure the highest quality product and presentation. Because we are committed to serving our readers' needs, we welcome your feedback on how we can improve future editions of this book.

Cover design by RIPE Creative, Inc.

Printed in the United States of America

Library of Congress Cataloging-in-Publication Data

Ellis, Jennifer, author.
  WordPress in one hour for lawyers / by Jennifer Ellis.
    pages cm
  Includes bibliographical references and index.
  ISBN 978-1-62722-210-5 (alk. paper)
  1. Internet in legal services--United States. 2. WordPress (Electronic resource) 3. Blogs--United States. 4. Social media--United States. 5. Lawyers--United States--Handbooks, manuals, etc. I. American Bar Association. Section of Law Practice Management, sponsoring body. II. Title.
  KF320.I57E45 2013
  006.7'802434--dc23

2013042529

Discounts are available for books ordered in bulk. Special consideration is given to state bars, CLE programs, and other bar-related organizations. Inquire at Book Publishing, American Bar Association, 321 N. Clark Street, Chicago, Illinois 60654.

www.ShopABA.org

Contents

About the Author

Jennifer Ellis is an attorney with the Philadelphia law firm of Lowenthal & Abrams, PC. She focuses her practice on issues involving social media as related to personal injury law. In addition, Jennifer manages the firm's online presence. Jennifer is also a law practice management consultant. Through her consulting, Jennifer aids law firms in creating and managing an online presence. A nationally recognized speaker and author, Jennifer lectures and writes on topics including social media, ethics, law practice management, and technology. She is the author of the book *WordPress in One Hour for Lawyers*, which instructs lawyers on how to create their own WordPress-based websites. Active in the Pennsylvania Bar Association, Jennifer is Secretary to the Solo and Small Firm Practice Section and the Gay and Lesbian Rights Committee. In addition, Jennifer is a member of the Law Practice Division of the American Bar Association, where she serves on the Publications and Diversity Committees.

Contact Jennifer at jennifer@jlellis.net and find her online at www.lowabram.com and www.jlellis.net.

Acknowledgments

There are a number of people I would like to thank. First and foremost would be my parents, who encouraged me to have an inquisitive mind and impressed on me the value of a great education. Second, I would like to thank everyone at the Pennsylvania Bar Institute, where I spent the first twelve years of my career. I learned a great deal from each and every person who worked there with me. I would like to especially thank Roger Meilton, who was in charge of PBI for the bulk of my tenure. Not only did Roger ask me to develop seminars on cutting edge issues of the law, but he encouraged me to speak and to develop my abilities as a lecturer and writer on technology, law and the Internet. It was through PBI that I met Sharon Nelson. After I left, Sharon encouraged me to become involved in the ABA and recommended me as a speaker at TECHSHOW. I am indebted to both she and John Simek for their support as I moved from the non-profit world to consulting and then a law firm. I would like to thank Ellen Freedman of both the Pennsylvania Bar Association and Freedman Consulting, for encouraging me to become a consultant. And I would like to thank Jeffrey Lowenthal and Dennis Abrams for asking me to join their firm. I also would like to thank Dennis Kennedy for reviewing the first draft of this book, and offering constructive suggestions for how I could improve it, as well as all the ABA Law Practice Division Publications Board for being supportive of the idea of this book. And last, but certainly not least, my thanks to the extraordinary ABA staff for helping me to create this publication.

Introduction

These days, a substantial number of people make decisions based on what they find on the web. This includes hiring a lawyer.[1] Law firms without websites are placing themselves at a great disadvantage compared with the competition. Even if you feel you receive the majority of your clients through referrals, a website provides the opportunity for those potential clients to learn about you and your firm.

I am always surprised when lawyers inform me that they do not have websites. It was due to my concern about the ability of solo and small-firm lawyers to compete with larger firms online that I decided to write this book. I would like to see all firms—solo, small, medium, or large—with websites that serve as professional, reliable online homes where lawyers can send their clients and where potential clients can find lawyers. To put it simply, the goal of this book is to explain exactly what you need to do to get your site up and running quickly and relatively painlessly using software called WordPress. Further, I explain the basic principles of search engine optimization (SEO) so you can be sure people will find your site once you create it, and I address ethical concerns so you can make certain your site adheres to the ethical rules that lawyers must follow for marketing.

The phrase "in One Hour" in the title of this book means that you should be able to read the book relatively quickly. Some might think the title means you can create a WordPress website in an hour. I do not believe

---

1   Amy Kovar, "New Study Finds Behavioral Shift in How Consumers Find Attorneys," *Blogs*, LexisNexis, September 25, 2012, http://tinyurl.com/cfx54ut/. The online search rate for Americans seeking a lawyer was 76 percent as of September 2012.

this is possible. Even with my experience with the program, unless I am doing something extremely simple, *I* cannot create a WordPress website in an hour. However, you can certainly produce a basic website in a morning, an afternoon, or over a weekend.[2]

The reason I recommend WordPress is because it is free and relatively easy to use. Free or inexpensive themes can enable a law firm to set up a website quickly and for very little cost. Plugins and widgets add a dizzying array of functionality, including helpful search engine optimization tools. Most important, if you use WordPress to create your website, you don't need to worry about hiring a third party to update the site. You can easily change text, add pictures, upload blog posts, and more. Once you become comfortable with WordPress, you will be able to maintain a high-quality, timely website that will help bring potential clients to your door.

A Note for the Basic User

If you are not used to coding or website design, that's OK; this book will still be useful. Focus on the basic steps now, get your website up and running, and worry about more complicated features later. My goal is to provide useful information for both beginners and those who are comfortable with technology.

If you are creating your first website, your best bet is to follow these steps:

1. Find a web host that offers one-click or automatic installation.
2. Use a theme that is free and that you can install quickly through the WordPress dashboard.
3. Make minimal edits to the theme.

---

2   Please keep in mind, your level of technological comfort will have a big impact on how long it takes you to set up your site. For a technically savvy person, building a site is a quick process. For someone with less experience, the process can take considerably longer.

4. Choose basic plugins to help you add functionality on the back end[3] of your site.

5. Choose basic widgets to add functionality on the front end[4] of your site.

6. Create a small number of pages and their content.

7. Write content, such as a new blog post, at least one a week.

If you do all of these things, you will be well on your way to a successful, professional-looking website to which you will be happy to point potential clients. Seem like a lot to do? It isn't. Read this book, and when you are finished you will be able to do all of these things and more. Over time, as you become more comfortable with WordPress, you will be able to make a more complicated website if you desire to do so.

---

3 Back end means the part of the website only you, as the owner, can see. In WordPress, the back end means the dashboard, which will be discussed later in the book.

4 Front end means the part of the website the public can see.

Choosing a Web Host

Before you can begin creating your website, you need to identify and purchase two important items. They are your web host and your domain name. Both of these pieces are extremely important, so it is crucial that you give them proper consideration.

The host is where your site sits on the web. Whenever you visit a website, you are actually visiting a server (or several servers) located somewhere in the world, and that server is normally owned by a host. Think of your server as the hard drive on your computer where you keep your files. This hard drive just happens to be accessible online and stored elsewhere.

Reliability and Speed

Given the importance of your web host, its reliability, speed, and ease of use are all vital. WordPress requires a host that is capable of handling its database-driven nature. Some hosts simply cannot handle a WordPress site properly. The wrong host will load your site very slowly, and people leave websites that are slow to load. No matter how wonderful your site turns out to be, if it doesn't load quickly, no one will stay around to look at it. Another issue with unreliable hosts is that they can crash. When the server on which your website is located crashes, if there is no backup and no rapid response from your host, your site could be down for hours or even days at a time. If people visit only to find an error page instead of content, you may have lost your chance to bring in potential new clients.

It comes down to this: with the wrong host, you can easily have a disaster on your hands, especially as your site becomes popular. So choose carefully.

Hosts I Recommend

Based on my own experiences and reviews by other people, there are three hosts I recommend. They are **Bluehost**,[5] **HostGator**,[6] and **Synthesis**.[7]

These three consistently appear as top-rated hosts for WordPress-based sites. Synthesis is specifically for WordPress—it does not host any other kind of website. The owners have a series of extremely successful WordPress sites. They decided to begin hosting to support them, later adding hosting services for others. Bluehost and HostGator offer one-click installation.[8] Synthesis already has WordPress installed when you begin. This means that with these hosts you do not have to worry about figuring out how to install the software, and you know it will be installed properly the first time.

It is important to remember that web hosts go through positive and negative times. Therefore, it is always a good idea to check rankings and reviews before you make your final decision. Given my own experiences, I find Bluehost and HostGator to be on par with each other. Synthesis costs

---

5 www.bluehost.com
6 www.hostgator.com
7 http://websynthesis.com
8 In reality, the installation will take several clicks, but the process is straightforward.

more but offers WordPress specialization. Generally speaking, you should be fine with any of these three hosts.

Picking Your Own Host

If you do not care about one-click installation and want to choose your own host, make sure that any host you pick has the basic requirements for a WordPress installation. As of the writing of this book, the requirements are as follows:

1. PHO version 5.2.4 or greater
2. MySQL version 5.0 or greater
3. Mod_Rewrite Apache Module

These requirements may change as WordPress evolves. If you do not know how to check if the listed items are available, you can e-mail the potential host and ask the following: "I would like to install WordPress on your service. Please tell me if [name of host] supports PHP 5.3.4 or greater, MySQL 5.0 or greater, and the mod_rewrite Apache module." If the answer is yes, you are good to go.

Note: Linux vs. Windows

When you purchase your hosting package, make sure you choose a Linux server as opposed to a Windows server. Many hosts will offer you this choice. If you make a mistake and choose the wrong server, or if you have already purchased a hosting package with Windows, ask your host if it can change you to Linux. This is necessary for installation of WordPress.

Note: Working with a Professional Web Designer

If you plan on working with a web designer, ask the designer what host he or she thinks is best. In the end, the main issue is simply to get WordPress running properly on a web host that is reliable and fast. Do not, however, be talked into putting your website on your designer's server, unless the designer can show you that he or she is using a host that is appropriate for a WordPress site. Many designers resell hosting services. The problem is that sometimes they are not using reliable hosts or they considerably mark up the service. It is appropriate to pay an additional fee if your designer includes managing the website for you, but the fee should be appropriate for the amount of work being provided each month.

Hosting Costs

Cost varies greatly among web hosts. Regardless of which host you choose, be certain that you pick a hosting package that's right for you. Your choice should not be the cheapest option. Look at a business-level or WordPress-specific package. There also might be some add-ons that can be useful. Bluehost and HostGator frequently offer discounts based on signing up for a long-term contract. The following prices are current as of the writing of this book.

Bluehost Pricing

Bluehost offers professional web hosting for $6.95 per month. It offers a $2 per month discount if you sign up for a year and pay in advance. For an additional fee, you can add backup, a dedicated IP address, and various other services. Some of these services are offered elsewhere, but a dedicated IP address can be a nice feature and can be added only through the host itself. My total cost in 2012 for one year of hosting, paid all at once, was $254.39.

HostGator Pricing

Currently, HostGator pricing for the Business Plan option ranges from $10.36 to $11.96 per month. You will need a separate backup system with HostGator.

Synthesis Pricing

Your price on Synthesis will vary based on how many sites you have and how much bandwidth you expect to need. Most people will begin with one site, and the amount of bandwidth in the Starter package will be enough. The cost is $27.00 per month. Synthesis provides the security service Sucuri for free, and it includes backup, but a secondary backup is never a bad idea.

Conclusion

It is unwise to be too focused on cost when you pick a host for your website. Choosing a host because it is included with some other service or because it is cheap is a bad idea. A host that cannot keep your website moving at a fast clip or that constantly crashes is going to cause you a lot of trouble and will not bring in clients.

Once you choose a host, you need to select a domain name to brand your firm and your website. In Lesson 2, I will provide information on identifying, purchasing, and setting up your domain name.

Choosing and Setting Up a Domain Name

A domain name is the address you type in a web browser to get to a specific website. The problem at this point is that many of the good domain names are taken; you might have to use some creativity to find one that works for you. There are several steps that go into choosing and checking a domain name before you begin to use it as the brand for your website.

Picking a Good Domain Name

A good domain name is extremely important. You should choose a domain name that is part of the overall branding of your law firm. Many SEO[9] experts used to recommend that you purchase several domain names, a few of which exactly matched some of your keywords. However, in the past year, Google began to penalize exact-match domain names that led to sites with poor content. While an exact-match domain name that leads to a site with good content is fine, the more important consideration is

---

9   SEO, or search engine optimization, relates to how easily people can find your website using a search engine, mainly Google. For more information, see Lesson 9.

having a domain name that works with your firm's overall branding. So think about the brand you are seeking to convey in both your off-line and online presence and go from there.

Use .com

Try to get a domain name with .com. People are familiar with .com, and that is what they will try to use to get to your website. If you have a different top-level domain,[10] people are likely to still type *.com*. It is generally better to choose a different domain name than to go with anything other than .com. For example, assume your law firm is named XYZ and you want the domain name XYZ.com. If XYZ.com is taken, consider registering XYZlaw.com instead. Flexibility is important when choosing the proper name.

Keep It Simple

Keep the name simple, short, and memorable. You want people to be able to type it quickly. Use the same domain name for your e-mail address. Do not use dashes or any other characters. Dashes add confusion and length to the name. If someone else has the same name but yours has a dash, people will consistently visit the other person's site instead of yours. Similarly, do not use numbers, unless your firm has a number in its name.

Watch for Competitors' Names

Be careful about using *my*, *the* (at the beginning), or *s* (at the end) to get around the fact that someone has the domain name you want—especially if the owner of that domain name is a competitor. When people forget

---

10 The top-level domain is the ending of your domain name, such as .com, .net, .org, and so on.

to type in the additional word or letter, they will end up at the competitor's site.

Relate the Domain Name to Your Brand

As already noted, make sure your domain name relates to the name and/ or brand of your firm. Many law firms use their initials. This is a fine idea, as long as the initials are available. Adding *law* or *lawfirm* to the end works well too, especially since it lets people know what your business is all about. The only problem is that years ago a number of businesses picked random initials and the word *law* and registered them. They are now in the business of selling those domain names. You might feel it is worth it to buy a name, if the cost is not prohibitive. I once had a client ask me to purchase such a name and ended up spending about $300 for it. Not much money in the grand scheme of things.

Some law firms use keywords, such as divorcelawyer.com. This is also acceptable and can be excellent for SEO, but it is very difficult to find short, concise names like this anymore.

Research the Name

You will need to do a search to see if your name is available. You can do so through your web host or virtually any domain name registrar. For example, if you decide to use HostGator as your host, when you begin the process of setting up your account, HostGator will ask you if you have a name already or want to choose one. If you respond that you need to choose one, HostGator will provide you with a tool to conduct a search.

You can access a domain search tool on pretty much any host. Just enter "domain name registrar" on Google.

1. Access a domain search tool.

2. Enter the name you would like. Most tools do not require you to type *.com*. Instead, you normally choose from a drop-down menu.

3. Click on **Search** to see the results. Most tools will offer recommendations if the desired name is not available. If the domain name you want is not available, keep searching until you find one that works for your firm.

Check What the Domain Name Might Spell

This may seem like a strange instruction, but sometimes we get so focused on what we think a domain name should be that we don't realize how other people might see it. In other words, it may not convey what we mean it to convey. A famous example is www.therapistfinder.org. Do you see *therapist finder* or *the rapist finder*? Obviously, this domain name is a problem.

Check for Prior Problematic Use

Just because a domain name is available now does not mean it has not been used in the past. Do a search on Google to see if the name comes up for anything offensive or problematic. For example, if you should want to use the name demonoid.com, you might be interested to know that Demonoid was a website that was famous for copyright infringement. It was a torrent site that enabled people to find illegal copies of music, movies, pictures, and so on. To check a name, do the following:

- Search the name in Google.

- Use the Internet Archive site's Wayback Machine to check for old versions of a site using the name.[11]

- Use URL Checker to find out the history of the domain name.[12]

---

11 The Wayback Machine (http://archive.org/index.php) archives old versions of websites.
12 http://www.netconcepts.com/urlcheck/

Check for Legal Issues

Make certain you are not violating someone else's trademark or causing yourself any other legal problems.

More Than One Domain Name to the Same Site

Some businesses will purchase all of the top-level domains for their chosen name, such as .net, .org, .biz, and so on, to protect themselves. This is fine if you are worried that someone else will take the domain name(s) and cause you trouble. You can own the names and have them actively lead to your site or simply turn them off. But do not purchase a huge number of domain names and have them all lead to your site. This can be harmful for your firm's SEO.[13]

In my case, I have both jlellis.net and jlellis.com. This makes sense because people might type either one to get to my site. For my law firm, we have both lowenthalabrams.com and lowenthalandabrams.com. Our main domain name is lowenthalabrams.com, but since we are actually called Lowenthal & Abrams, people might be inclined to type the latter.

How to Purchase Your Domain Name

You can choose to purchase[14] your domain name on your web host or on a different registrar;[15] it is up to you. Sometimes web designers will purchase the domain name in one location and host the website with another company. This is to avoid putting all of their eggs in one basket.

---

13 See Lesson 9 on SEO for more information about domain names.

14 It is not truly accurate to use the word *purchase* or *buy* when talking about obtaining a domain name, but that is generally the word everyone uses. In reality, you are actually renting the name. You may rent it for up to ninety-nine years at a time.

15 A domain name registrar is a company that manages your domain name for you and reports it to the registration network of all domain names. This prevents others from purchasing the same name.

On the other hand, it is easy to keep the domain name in the same location as the host, since the domain name will already be set to work with the host. In the end, it is entirely your choice whether to register your domain name in the same place you host your site. I have sites where the domain name is registered in the same location as the web host and sites where they are separate.[16] As far as registrars, there are many that work quite well. I recommend the following: HostGator, Bluehost, GoDaddy, and BulkRegister.

Price of and Purchase of a Domain Name

The cost of purchasing a domain name can vary greatly. Some sites offer a deal on the first domain name you purchase with a new hosting package, perhaps offering it for free for the first year or even permanently. Others charge a few dollars. Generally speaking, I find the cost of a .com domain name ranges from around $6.00 to $15.00 per year.

The purchase process is easy. If you are using your web host to purchase your domain name, buy it when you set up your hosting package. If you want a different domain name registrar, run your search and the registrar's site will walk you through the process.

How Long to Register the Name?

You often can save money by buying the domain name for several years at once. Many sites include an automatic renewal service. This is a very good idea, since you do not want to find your domain name attached to someone else's website or your website down because you forgot to renew your name.

---

16 If you choose Synthesis as your host, you will need a different registrar. Synthesis does not offer registrar services.

Setting Up the Domain Name

How you set up your domain name will depend on whether you registered the name with your web host and whether your e-mail runs through that host or a different service.

If your domain name is with the same host as your website, it will initially be set up to work with your website and nothing more will need to be done. If you choose a separate registrar and host, you will need to point what is called the DNS[17] from the registrar to the website. The DNS tells your registrar where to send web traffic when someone types in your domain name. A DNS looks something like this: dns1.webhostname.com.

You should use at least two DNS designations. (You will be provided with two.) One serves as a backup for the other in case something goes wrong. Your web host will give you the DNS information for your site during setup. You simply need to save that information and put it into the right place on your registrar.[18] That location will vary based on the particular registrar. Most of the time, if you run a Google search for "DNS Setup [Name of registrar]" you will find good instructions. Otherwise, check with your web host and your registrar for directions.

Note: If you work with a web designer, insist on purchasing your own domain name and putting it in your own account over which you have control. While most web designers are very reputable, I have run into cases where a lawyer and a designer had a falling out, the domain name was registered in the designer's name, and the designer refused to turn it over to the lawyer. Generally speaking, the person whose name is on the domain

---

17 DNS stands for Domain Name System or Server (both are correct). The DNS lets the Internet know where a domain name should send a user when it is typed into a web browser. Essentially, the DNS translates your domain name into the numerical address where your website is actually located on the web.

18 If you are hosting your e-mail in a separate location, you will need the IP address of the site instead of the DNS information. The IP address is a series of numbers that identifies where the site is located.

name owns it. There are ways to fight this, but meanwhile, you have lost your website and probably your e-mail. It isn't work the risk.

Conclusion

It is vital to pick a good domain name that relates to your law firm as a brand. Because your domain name is not only your home on the web but also part of your e-mail address, this piece of branding will often be what sticks in your clients' minds about you. Spend some time and pick a name that works well for your firm. You won't want to change it later.

Now that you have your domain name and a host, you are ready to begin working with WordPress. Lesson 3 covers how to install and set up the basic aspects of the software.

Lesson 3

Installing and Setting Up WordPress

If you follow my recommendation and choose a host that allows one-click installation of WordPress, the actual installation process will be quite straightforward.[19] If you choose Synthesis, WordPress will already be installed and you can skip directly to the setup.

Installing WordPress with One-Click Installation

If you choose a host that has a one-click WordPress installation, simply locate where you begin the installation and go through the process.[20] If the host asks you where you want to install WordPress, choose the root directory, assuming it will be driving your entire website. If you already have a website and just want to use WordPress as a blog, then you can install it in a secondary directory. The root directory would be, for example, www.jlellis.net. A subdirectory would be www.jlellis.net/blog, with /blog being the subdirectory.

---

19 See Appendix C for instructions on installing WordPress on your own.
20 If at any point you run into problems, contact your host's technical support.

After the process is complete, you can start setting up the basic components of WordPress for your website.

Setting Up WordPress

Now that WordPress is installed on your host, it is time to begin choosing the basic settings. You will see one of two screens, depending on the type of install.

Either you will see a screen asking you to provide a title, username, password, and e-mail address, as in Figure 3.1, or you will see the WordPress Dashboard, as in Figure 3.2. If you see Figure 3.1, simply complete the information. Frequently, the username will be already filled in as "Admin." Please do not keep this as your username. Hackers have recently focused on WordPress websites using Admin as a username.

Figure 3.1 WordPress Welcome Screen

Figure 3.2 Dashboard Welcome Screen

Site Name/Blog Title

WordPress refers to the site name as Blog Title, but in this case it means the same thing. Pick a name that makes sense. My law firm's site is called Lowenthal & Abrams, PC. My website is called Jennifer Ellis, JD.

The site name will automatically appear in each post or page you create, though you can override this. The good news is if you do not like your name, you can change it later.

Username

You can have more than one username; you simply are picking the first name to control your site. You will probably use this name to post on your site, so it will be publicly associated with it. Choose a name that makes sense. Again, please do not use Admin.[21]

---

21 If you use Synthesis as your host, the username will be Admin. You will be required to click on **Lost Password** and then set up a new password to begin working on your site. At that point, create a new username. Make it an administrator, and then, once you are sure you have set up the new username correctly, you can

You cannot change a username, but you can create additional names and delete old ones. If you delete a name, be careful you do not delete by mistake all the content you created under that name. When you delete a name, if you created posts or other content under that name, you will be asked if you want to assign the content to a different username. Choose a new name and apply the content to that name so you will not lose it.

Password

A strong password is crucial. WordPress sites are constantly under attack by hackers. Weak passwords are easily broken, and then your site is in the hands of nefarious people who can do whatever they choose with it, often without your knowledge. Frequently, those people will install malware to harm your visitors, which can get your site blacklisted.[22] They can also replace or delete all of your content. So, please, choose a strong password.

A strong password comprises at least ten characters. I prefer thirteen or fourteen. Those characters should be a mixture of uppercase and lowercase letters, numbers, and special characters such as ! and @. The password should not spell out anything. In the old days, I would recommend taking a word and replacing certain letters with numbers and characters, such as P@55W0rD! But this just does not cut it anymore. Hackers easily break into such accounts. You should also never use a password that is somehow related to you. Your birthday, kids' birthdays, place of marriage, and other personal information can be found online.

The best way to choose a password is to use a random password creator. An excellent one can be found at http://www.pctools.com/guides/password/.

---

delete the Admin username. *Do not* delete the Admin username until you are positive you have set up the new username correctly, or you will be unable to access your site.

22 A site that is blacklisted means it shows up on Google and other search engines with a warning that it is not safe. If someone clicks on the link, the person will again see a warning that the site is not safe. Getting blacklisted is a serious problem for a website.

Adjust the number of characters, since currently the site is set to eight. You should change it to fourteen.

The Dashboard

The control panel through which you operate the back end of your Word-Press website is called the Dashboard. From here you will create content, design your site, manage comments from visitors, and more. Do not be concerned that your website's Dashboard looks different from mine, shown in Figure 3.3 below. I have numerous features installed on my website that you may or may not choose to include.

Figure 3.3 WordPress Dashboard

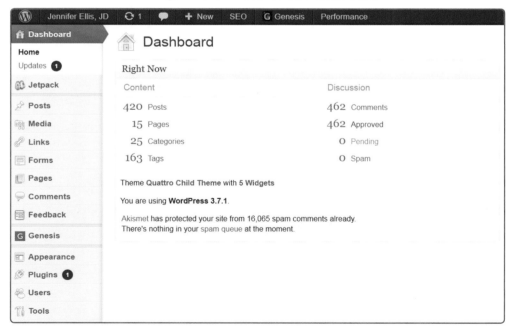

Access the Dashboard

There are two ways to access your Dashboard. First, some WordPress sites are designed to include a login link. You can login through that link. Otherwise, access the Dashboard by typing www.yourdomainname.com/wp-admin or www.yourdomainname.com/wp-login to access your Dashboard. If you have installed your website on a subdirectory, do not forget to include that in your link; that is, www.yourdomainname.com/directory/wp-admin.[23]

Basic Settings

Your first use of the Dashboard will be to walk through the basic settings that control what visitors see on your website and how they communicate with you through the site. Begin with the six tabs on the left of the Dashboard. Click on the tab called *Settings* and you will see the list shown in Figure 3.4.

Figure 3.4 Basic WordPress Settings

General

The general settings are pretty straightforward, as you can see in Figure 3.5. Here, you will review the title of your site as well as your tagline. In a basic WordPress setup, the tagline will show, but on many sites it is hidden. If you do not want a tagline, simply leave this blank.

---

23 A common WordPress bug involves the admin panel redirecting to another link (still on your site) and giving you a login error. If this happens, return to the login page and try again. If you are not sure you are typing your password correctly, reset it.

Do not change the WordPress address URL or the site address URL unless you know what you are doing, or you will seriously mess up your site.

This page is also where you can change your e-mail address if you ever need to do so. Please make sure that you use a current e-mail address here. If you should ever forget your password, you will need access to this e-mail address to reset it.

Under Membership, you are deciding who can register on your site. If you want people to be able to subscribe to your site, allow registration. If you do not, uncheck the box.

The time zone and date settings are self-explanatory. Choose whichever applies to you.

When you are finished, click **Save Changes**.

Figure 3.5 General Settings

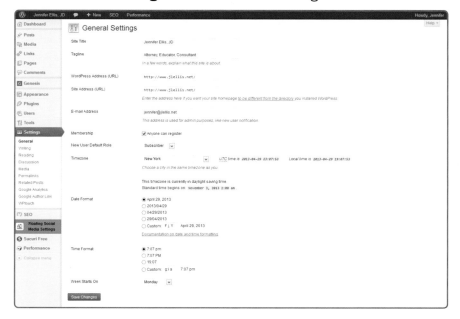

Writing

The writing settings (see Figure 3.6) control a few minor issues. Here you can choose your default post category (more about categories later) and set up the ability to post via e-mail.

Figure 3.6 Writing Settings

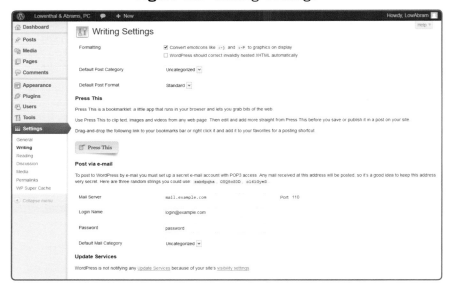

Reading

In the reading settings (see Figure 3.7), you control how information is displayed on your website for readers.

Figure 3.7 Reading Settings

If you plan on making your WordPress installation your entire website, then you will need to change the **Front page displays** option from **Your latest posts** to **A static page**. To do this, you will need to first create a new page to serve as your home page. I will discuss creating new pages in more detail in lesson 8, but here is what you need to do to create a basic page. Steps 3 through 6 are shown in Figure 3.8.

1. Hover your mouse over **Pages**.
   a. Click *Add New*.
   b. At the top, where it reads **Enter title here**, name your page. For your home page, it is best to name it Home, Welcome, or Index.
   c. Click *Publish*.
2. You will also need to create a blog page. Repeat the above steps, but name the

Figure 3.8 Creating a Basic WordPress Page

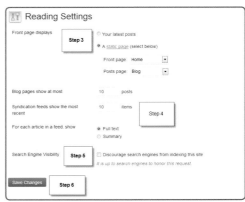

page Blog or News or whatever you want your blog page to be known as.

    a. Be careful not to actually enter any text in the body of the blog page, or it will not work properly.

3. Return to ***Reading Settings***.

    a. Choose ***A static page***.

    b. Choose the page you created to be your front page under **Front Page**.

    c. Choose the page you created for your blog under **Posts Page**.

4. The next part deals with how many posts show on your blog and how those posts appear.

    a. Choose how many blog posts you want to show at a time on your blog page.

    b. Choose how many blog post titles will appear in the RSS feed for your site.[24]

    c. Choose whether you want to show the full text of your blog posts or a summary.

5. The Search Engine Visibility option controls whether search engines can find your site. While you are working on your site, before you are ready for the public to see it, you might want to check this box. Otherwise, keep it unchecked or it will be all but impossible for anyone to find your website. That, of course, would defeat the purpose.

6. Click on ***Save Changes*** when you are done.

---

24 RSS stands for Really Simple Syndication. This is a form of news feed that you can show on your site, or that other people can subscribe to and show on their own websites. In 4b you are choosing the number of your posts which will appear in feed.

Discussion

Discussion is where you control whether you will allow people to comment on your blog posts. This is entirely up to you. That said, I encourage allowing comments. The more interaction you are able to receive, the better. People are also more likely to link to you if they are able to comment. Generally, I suggest you leave everything as is for now; you can always change it later.

You can block certain words or addresses in the box near the bottom of the page (see Figure 3.9).

Figure 3.9 Discussion Settings

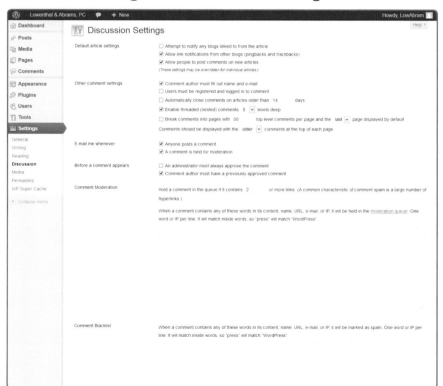

Media

This page (Figure 3.10) is where you control the default for uploading of pictures to your site. I recommend you leave it as is.

Figure 3.10 Media Settings

Permalinks

Permalinks are important for SEO purposes, so make sure you review these settings before you start posting on your site. Permalinks control what shows up in your links, and link names are very important. There are a variety of ways you can set your permalinks (see Figure 3.11). I recommend that you at least use the post name, and you might want to add a date too. Click the option(s) that you want and then click **Save Changes**.

Figure 3.11 Permalinks Settings

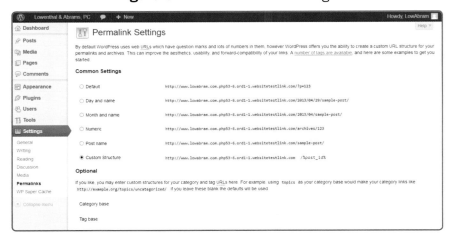

Updates and Backups

It is crucial to keep WordPress up-to-date. When an update has been released, you will see a message on your Dashboard. To perform the update, you need only click on the link and follow the directions. Before you perform the update, please be certain to back up your site. You should have several types of backups, which I mention throughout this book.

1. A web host that provides a backup (Some web hosts, such as Bluehost and Synthesis, provide automatic backups.)

2. A backup service (Jetpack, which I discuss in Lesson 6 on plugins, has a service called VaultPress. You can use it to perform backups.)

3. Export the content (You can export the content—though not the design—of your site through WordPress itself: **Tools > Export > All Content > Download Export File.**)

Conclusion

As you move through the steps of the initial WordPress settings, remember that they can be changed later. Be careful not to change anything that will alter links, such as permalinks, because this will cause any links that you have shared with people to change. However, it is fine to make changes like this before your site is launched.

Now that WordPress is set up, the next step is to decide how your site will look. This involves choosing what is called a theme. I will address the various options for finding themes in Lesson 4.

Choosing the Look of Your Website

Once you have installed WordPress and set up some initial information, including the title of the site and how the basic back end tools will work, it is time to decide what your site will look like. The first step in doing so is picking the scheme of colors and layout for your site. In WordPress, this is called a theme.

My main advice for picking a theme comes down to this:

- Make certain the theme pleases you. If you do not like your website, you will not work with it and will not want to share it with other people.

- Choose a theme that will allow you to modify it in line with your needs or desires in terms of how your site will look.

- Make sure the theme is easy to use and easy for visitors to navigate. If people cannot easily explore the content on your site, they will become frustrated and leave it.

- Pick a theme that fits your brand. Your website should be professional and fit in with the overall impression you want to convey to your clients.

- Consider using a theme that is mobile responsive. Mobile responsive themes automatically adjust depending on what the viewer is using to look at your site. If you use a mobile responsive theme, you will not have to worry about creating a mobile site or adding any plugins to create mobile functionality.

Finding a Theme

There are several ways you can go about locating a theme. The price and time commitment, as well as the results, will vary greatly depending on how you decide to go.

Free Themes

WordPress contains numerous free themes that you can use to get your site up and running quickly. Some of the themes allow for a great deal of flexibility, giving you a lot of control over what your site will look like; others do not. Some of the themes are quite attractive and professional; others are less so.

Accessing the free themes is quite simple. Begin by clicking on the **Appearance** tab on your Dashboard. Then click on **Themes**. You will see a tab reading **Manage Themes** and another reading **Install Themes**. The page you will see first will be your Manage Themes page, and it will show any themes already installed on your site. In most cases, you will see a theme called **Twenty Twelve**, which is the default WordPress theme.

To search for and install free themes, click on the **Install Themes** tab (see Figure 4.1). From here you can begin the search process.

Figure 4.1 Installing a Free Theme

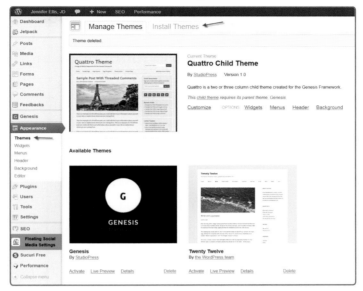

Check the appropriate boxes to limit your search. Categories are shown in Figure 4.2.

Figure 4.2 Theme Search

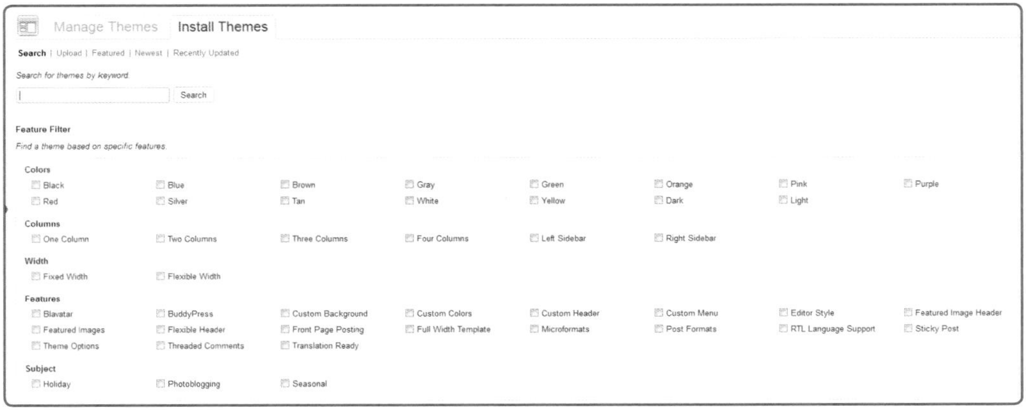

If you want to have more control over your theme, you will want to pick a few options right from the start. Those options might include the following:

- Custom Header, which will enable you to choose or create a header for the top of your website
- Custom Background, which will allow you to control the background color or image for your site
- Custom Colors, which will allow you to change the various colors of your site

If you pick a theme you do not like, it is easy to change, so do not hesitate to install a lot of different themes until you find the right one for you.

Once you begin your search, you will see thumbnails of each theme. Click on **Preview** to see what a theme looks like. Click ***Install*** to install it. A sample preview page is shown in Figure 4.3.

Figure 4.3 Theme Preview Page

Once you install a theme, you can click **Live Preview** to see more, or you can activate it to make it the theme for your site. You can also activate a theme you previously installed by returning to the Theme page and clicking on **Activate**, as shown in Figure 4.4.

Figure 4.4 Activating a Theme

Find Themes Online

There are numerous themes available on the web. The quality of these themes varies greatly. You can find options simply by searching for WordPress themes on Google. The prices will vary as much as the capability of the designers. Check and see if the person who created the theme provides updates for it and offers any kind of support.

Note: Make sure the theme is from a reputable designer. Improperly designed themes can have security holes. Some themes can be set up to spread malware.

Installing a theme you purchase is a bit different from simply searching on WordPress and clicking some buttons, but it is not complicated. Steps 3 and 4 are shown in Figure 4.5.

1. Purchase and download the theme.
2. Access the Theme page.
3. Click on the **Install Themes** tab.
4. Click **Upload**.

Figure 4.5 Installing a Purchased Theme

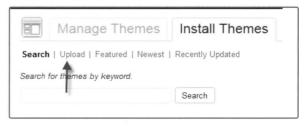

5. Browse to where you downloaded the theme.

6. Upload it.

The rest of the steps are exactly the same as when you install a theme you found on WordPress.

Hire Someone to Create a Theme

There are many WordPress designers. You can hire someone to create a theme just for you. Fees will vary. Talk with designers of WordPress themes who offer the service and find out how much they charge. Determine how much control you will have over the design and whether they are writing the theme from scratch or modifying an existing theme.

Use a Theme Tool

There are a number of tools out there that enable you to begin with a relatively advanced theme and then modify it to whatever degree makes you happy. This is actually how I design websites. The tool I use is called Genesis. There are numerous themes that work with the Genesis Framework, or you can use Framework and have a personalized theme designed for you on top of it. The benefit to using Genesis is that the Framework is constantly updated, while a site designed completely from scratch might not receive appropriate updates. You can purchase Genesis and one theme (or several themes) and then modify the theme as you desire. The cost for the Genesis Framework and one theme is currently $59 to $99.[25]

Using Genesis is a little more complicated than buying and uploading a theme, but it's still doable for someone new to WordPress. The difference is that there are two parts to install instead of just one. Genesis itself is the first part, and the theme is the second part. You will need both.

---

25 http://my.studiopress.com/themes/genesis/

1. Download the Genesis Framework and the theme you chose from the website.

2. Install the Genesis Framework (*Theme > Install > Upload > Activate*).

3. Install the theme itself (*Theme > Install > Upload > Activate*).

Once you install Genesis, you will see a new item on your Dashboard for working with the Framework, as shown in Figure 4.6. Genesis is my favorite method for creating and designing WordPress websites. I find the results are often the most professional looking of the self-designed or inexpensively designed sites.

Figure 4.6 Theme Tool

Note: Updating Your Theme

If you install a theme from the WordPress Dashboard or another site that provides automatic updates, please be certain to update your theme whenever an update is released. You will see a note informing you that an update is available. Depending on the theme, you will be provided a link to immediately update it or you will need to access your Theme page and click on ***Update***.[26]

If your website is designed by a third party, make sure you find out if any updates are being created and get them installed. Failure to keep your theme up-to-date can result in security holes or functionality problems for your site.[27]

If you experimented with a lot of themes, please be sure to delete the themes you will not be using. Old themes that are not updated can leave holes for malware to be installed on your site.

Conclusion

The nice thing about WordPress is that it is easy to try out different themes until you find the one you like. In addition, the themes can be modified. How much they can be modified depends on the design of the theme and your own comfort level with making modifications.

Now that you have chosen your basic theme, it is time to learn how to make changes to it, such as choosing a header that matches your firm branding. How to do this and more is covered in Lesson 5.

---

26 Back up your site by exporting it before you install an update.
27 See Lesson 10 on ethics for more information.

Manipulating a Theme

After you install and activate a theme, you can edit it. There are two ways to edit a theme. The way you will want to do it is to use the tools within WordPress. Otherwise, you will have to go into the actual code of the theme, which for the average person is probably unwise. If you change the code and don't know what you are doing, you can easily break your site.

Assuming you want to avoid actually editing code, what you can and cannot change will vary based on the theme you choose. In some cases, you will be able to change almost nothing. In other cases, you will be able to change colors, but will be limited to some specific choices. In still other cases, you will be able to change virtually anything you desire. You need to choose a theme that allows for the level of customization you want.[28]

Manage Themes Page

To control the design of your theme, access **Appearance** and **Themes** on the Dashboard. Here you will see the various options allowed by the theme you installed. Click on whatever item you want to edit in this section. My theme is called Quattro Child. As you can see in Figure 5.1, I can customize a number of options, including the header and background.

---

28 See Lesson 4.

Figure 5.1 Customizing the Theme

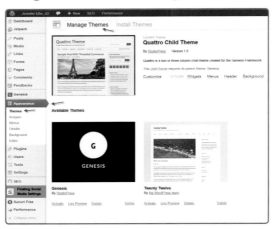

If you want to change the header, click on ***Header***, and you will be taken to a page that allows you to add or remove an image and change the text, the color, and so on. Again, whether you can do all of these things will depend on the theme you choose. The header on my website is actually just plain text. But if I wanted to use a graphic instead, I could create that graphic, make sure it is the correct size, and upload it in place of my current header.

Creating a Header for Your Theme

You can create a header or any other graphics for your theme using a number of software programs. I am not a graphic artist, so I tend to keep my graphics simple and work with a program called Snagit. A graphic artist is more likely to use Adobe Photoshop or some other more intense program.

Let's say I would like a header that suggests technology in some way. I have an image that I want to use, to which I want to add the company name. In my case, I will open the file in the Snagit editor so I can shrink it to the appropriate size and add some text. I must keep in mind what the final size of my image needs to be. (This will vary, based on the chosen theme.) In my case, the image is supposed to be 1100 x 120 pixels. If I make it too large, I will need to crop it when I upload it. Once I have completed the image, I will go to back to the Theme page and click on *Header*, then click on *Browse* and navigate my way to the image I created (see Figure 5.2).

I made the image the correct length but left it too wide, so now I have to crop it. I can move the image around and crop it as I like. When I am done, I click *Crop and Publish* (see Figure 5.3).

Figure 5.3 Crop and Publish

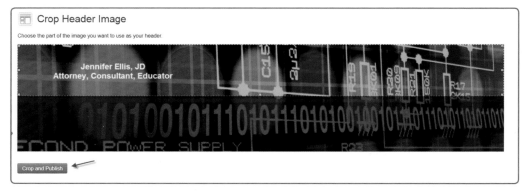

As you can see in Figure 5.4, the image still has the original text overlapping my new text. This means I need to remove the old text. To do this, I scroll down and click the check box for *Show header text with your image*.

Figure 5.4 Removing Original Text from an Image

This resolves the problem, and my new header (Figure 5.5) is ready.

Figure 5.5 Sample Customized Header

If I do not like the result, I return to the Header page and click ***Restore Original Header Image*** (see Figure 5.6). This returns the site to its default, which in this theme's case is plain text.

Figure 5.6 Restoring the Original Header Image

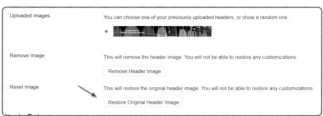

Changing Background Color or Image

As with changing the header, your ability to change the background color depends on the theme you choose. In some cases, you will be able to change the color, and in others you will not.

Generally, and depending on your theme, there are two ways to set a background color. One is to create an image and use that as your background. The image can be a solid color or something else—whatever you like, really. You can also set the color by choosing a color that pleases you directly from the theme.

Creating an Image

Creating an image to serve as the background of your website is the same as creating a header. Find or create an image (Figure 5.7), edit it to fit the frame of your site, and upload it. Upload your image by clicking browse, finding the correct image on your computer, and then clicking upload. It takes a lot more work to design a nice-looking background that

Figure 5.7
Create Custom Background

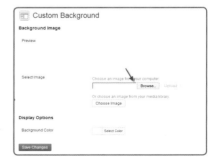

is an actual image as opposed to just making it a color. Your mileage will vary based on your graphic design and layout abilities.

Changing the Color

If you prefer to just change the color of the background, use the Background Color tool, shown in Figure 5.8. Simply try different colors until you find one you like. You can always change the color back, so there is no harm in experimenting.

Figure 5.8
Background Color Tool

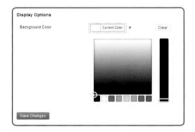

Note: Finding Images

You can download free or inexpensive graphics from various sites on the web. A free site that works well is called morgue-File.[29] There are numerous pay sites that you can use to find nice-looking images; I frequently use Shutterstock.[30] If you are or know a good photographer, you can get photos that way as well. Whatever you do, please do not just run a Google image search to find photos or images. You will end up violating copyright and that can get very expensive.

Conclusion

One of the nice things about WordPress is that themes can be altered quite easily. Like painting your home, you can easily change the color of your site, if the theme allows for it. If not, you can hire someone, at relatively

---

29 http://www.morguefile.com/
30 http://www.shutterstock.com

low cost, to change the color for you. If you hire someone who can code, there is little about most WordPress themes that cannot be altered.

In addition to the ease of setting up a basic WordPress website, a lot of functionality can be added to both the back and front end of the site through applications called plugins. Plugins take the place of coding and help with things such as speeding up your site, protecting you from malware, and stopping spam comments from wasting your time. I will address these tools in Lesson 6.

Adding Functionality through Plugins

Plugins are tools coded by people who want to help improve the functionality of WordPress. Some do this for free, some ask for a donation, and others might require payment. It is important to understand that badly written plugins can slow down your site, so be sure to pick plugins that are well reviewed and frequently updated.

Virtually anything you can think of to add to your site has probably already been thought of by someone else, who created a plugin for it. The way to find out is to search through the WordPress plugin tool or to search the web generally.

The theme you choose is, in some cases, directly related to what plugins you might need. You may want to wait to add design-related plugins until you have worked out the theme and determined what functionality you want to add to your site. You can also install plugins in the beginning and remove them later, if you desire. They can always be uninstalled.[31]

---

31 The caveat is that if a plugin is required to run part or all of your site, uninstalling it can break your site. Be careful about randomly uninstalling plugins if you are not sure what they do and if you are not sure it is safe to do so.

Installing Plugins

Installing plugins that are available from within WordPress is pretty straightforward. Each step below is accompanied by a screenshot of the WordPress page on which it appears (Figures 6.1–6.4).

1. Access the **Plugins** tab on the left side of the Dashboard.

   a. Click on *Add New*.

Figure 6.1 Add New

   b. Search for the plugin you want to add.

Figure 6.2 Search

c. Find the correct plugin and click ***Install Now***.

Figure 6.3 Install

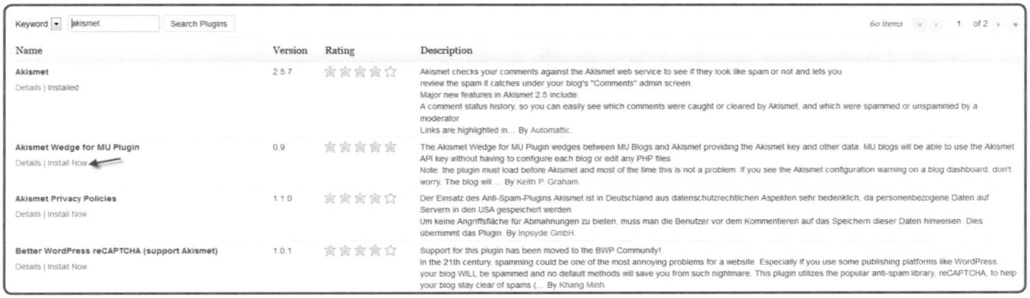

d. Click on ***Activate*** when the installation is completed.

Figure 6.4 Activate

Plugins I Recommend

Akismet

Akismet is crucial if you are going to allow comments on your blog. It helps control spam. Any blog that is even a little bit successful is going to be inundated with spam comments. Once you download and activate Akismet, you will be asked for a key. Create the key by following the instructions (you will need to provide an e-mail address to set it up). Once everything is set up correctly, you will see a series of green boxes.

WordPress SEO by Yoast

While WordPress on its own has some great SEO functionality, there is no doubt in my mind that WordPress SEO is the best SEO plugin out there. Install it and use its tools to make certain you have the proper SEO for your site.[32]

Display Widgets

The Display Widgets plugin allows you to control what widgets show up on various

Figure 6.5 Akismet Key Configuration

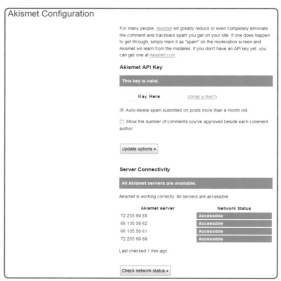

pages. For example, if you want the archive of your blog posts to show up on your blog, archive, and error pages but not on the rest of your website, you can use Display Widgets to control this. How you design your site will impact whether you need Display Widgets. This is the plugin I use to control how my website looks in terms of showing different widgets on different pages.[33]

Jetpack by WordPress.com

WordPress.com is where you can host a WordPress site for free. I do not recommend using it as the host for your professional site, because it has some limitations. However, there are some benefits to creating a connection from your website to a Wordpress.com account through the Jetpack plugin. This plugin has a lot of very useful tools. Once you download

---

32 See Lesson 9.
33 See Lesson 7 on using Display Widgets in combination with a widget.

the plugin, you will need to connect your website to WordPress.com. To do so, you need to create a WordPress.com account. Once you connect your Website to a WordPress.com account, you can control the settings of Jetpack by hovering your mouse over the Jetpack option that will appear on your Dashboard.

Figure 6.6 Jetpack

As you can see in Figure 6.6, there are quite a few items you can set up via Jetpack. Choose whichever make sense for you. I tend to use the following:

- **WordPress.com Stats** is a great tool for seeing how many people are visiting your site. It also provides other information. I like it because it is easy to interpret.
- **Publicize** connects your site to some social media sites. It allows for automatic sharing of posts on those sites.
- **Subscriptions** enables people to subscribe to posts and comments.
- **Spelling and Grammar** checks your spelling and grammar.

- **Enhanced Distribution** increases the reach of your website.
- **Jetpack Comments** is an improved comment tool that integrates the ability to log in to your site through social media.

The following are tools I sometimes use in Jetpack, depending on the circumstances:

- **Contact Form** is a potential contact form to use on your site. Contact forms are often an issue in WordPress, and this form may be a good solution.
- **WP.me Shortlinks** offers an easy way to obtain shorter links for sharing.
- **Notifications** provides a way to constantly be reminded of what is going on with your site.
- **VaultPress** is an excellent backup tool if you need one for your site. It costs $20 per month.
- **Mobile Theme** is one option for creating a version of your site that shows well on phones and tablets. I generally use other options, but this is also a good choice.

Jetpack frequently adds new tools, so check regularly to see what is available and if it will be useful for your site.[34]

Disable Comments

Depending on how you code your blog—that is, what tools you use to create it—you might need to hide comments on your pages. If you do not hide comments, your website will look very sloppy, with the comment

---

34 As I was finalizing this book, Jetpack added a feature that can replace the Display Widgets plugin. I cannot comment on it because I do not like to recommend plugins and widgets until I have had a chance to use them for quite a while. But this feature is an option to consider.

box not only on your blog posts but also on your formal pages. This is something I see a lot with people designing their own WordPress websites. Disable Comments allows you to choose where the comment box shows and helps make your site look more professional.

Once you install and activate Disable Comments, you will need to configure it. To do so, go to the *Settings* tab and click on *Disable Comments*, which will be there after you install the plugin (see Figure 6.7). I recommend you disable comments on pages and media. Leave posts alone, or you will prevent people from commenting on your blog posts. If you do not want comments anywhere on your website, disable all comments directly from the **Settings** panel, as discussed in Lesson 3.

Figure 6.7 Disable Comments

Only install the Disable Comments plugin if it is necessary to your site. You will know it is necessary if you look at a page and see the comments box (shown at the bottom of Figure 6.8).

Figure 6.8 Comments Box

Acurax Social Icons

As part of your online presence, you should set up a Facebook page, Google+ page, Twitter account, and more. You should then make it easy for people to access your accounts and pages from your website. Acurax Social Icons is a great plugin for this purpose. Once you install it, you will see a bright green box on the left side of your Dashboard called **Floating Social Media Settings**. Click on it to enable the settings, which are shown in Figure 6.9. You can choose the Premium (pay) or free version, depending on your needs. Decide on the theme you prefer, fill out your various social media feeds (you will get that information from the specific accounts and pages), and organize the order of your icons.[35]

---

35 See Lesson 7 for how to make social media icons appear on your website.

Figure 6.9 Floating Social Media Settings

Google Author Link

You should set up both an individual (personal) Google+ account and a Google+ business page for your firm. Once you do so, you will want to connect the Google+ personal account to your blog. This is an extremely valuable SEO tool. An easy way to make the connection is with **Google Author Link** (Figure 6.10).

Figure 6.10 Google Author Link

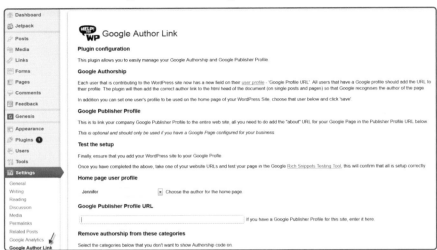

What you need to do is put a link to your website in your Google+ profile. This would be in your About page, which should be similar to the one shown in Figure 6.11.

Figure 6.11 Google+ About Page

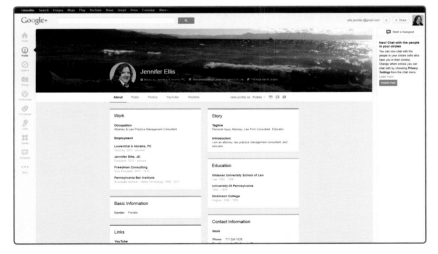

Once you have completed this, choose the name of the user who is posting to your site as your author under **Home page user profile** (see Figure 6.10 above). This will be the username under which you log in to the site and post your blog.

You should do the same for your business page, except the information goes in the **Google Publisher Profile URL** box (see Figure 6.10 above). Simply copy and paste the URL from the business page, as shown in Figure 6.12.

Figure 6.12 Google Publisher URL

W3 Total Cache

People expect to be able to navigate websites quickly. If your website is too slow, users will head away from it faster than you can say "lost client." W3 Total Cache, shown in Figure 6.13, helps with this problem by speeding up your site. Begin by using the default settings. The plugin starts in a preview mode, so you will need to turn it on. W3 Total Cache will add a tab called **Performance** to your Dashboard. You control the plugin through that tab. Be careful working with the W3 plugin because some settings can cause problems for your site. Research any settings you plan on altering. Some hosts, such as Synthesis, require specific settings. Synthesis gives you a list of its recommended settings should you choose to use this plugin.

Figure 6.13 W3 Total Cache

Gravity Forms

Creating a contact form can be a bit difficult on WordPress. I actually spent a lot of time trying various forms, with many different results. There are positives and negatives to each form type. The tool that most professional web designers use now is called Gravity Forms.[36] Unlike many of the other form options, Gravity Forms is not free, but in my opinion it is worth the cost. The fee is $39 for one website, which includes one year of support. The Gravity Forms plugin enables you to create a basic contact form (Figure 6.14) or build your own customized form.

---

36 http://www.gravityforms.com/purchase-gravity-forms/

Google Analyticator

Google provides tools to help you analyze how your website is performing. The tools together are called Google Analytics. To use Google Analytics you will first need to sign up for an account. There are a number of plugins, such as Jetpack, which provide some detail, but Google Analytics provides more. As a result, it is very useful to set up a Google Analytics account to work with a plugin such as Google Analyticator.

Figure 6.14
Gravity Forms Contact Form

1. If you do not have a Google Analytics account for your website, sign up at http://www.google.com/analytics/.

2. Next, you need to set up the code to work with your website.

   a. Click on ***Admin***.

   b. Click on ***New Account***.

   c. Fill out the information for your website on the form shown in Figure 6.16.

   d. Click ***Get Tracking ID***.

Then you need to set up Google Analyticator (or another plugin that works with Google Analytics and shows on your Dashboard):

1. Locate and install the Google Analyticator plugin.

2. Activate the plugin.

3. You will see a message that you must set up Analyticator and provide an ID.

a. There are two ways to provide the ID. One is automatic. Try this option first. Your site will ask permission to access your Google Analytics account. Grant it permission and allow it to complete the setup.

b. If the first way does not work, copy your tracking ID from your Google Analytics account and paste it into the appropriate box.

4. To access the stats, start on the Dashboard home screen.

5. Click on **Screen Options**.

6. Make sure **Google Analytics Summary** is checked (see Figure 6.17).

Figure 6.16 Account Administration

Figure 6.17 Google Analytics Summary

Genesis Plugins

If you decide to use Genesis, there are several plugins you might find useful.

Simple Edits and Simple Hooks are two plugins that serve similar purposes. Both make it easier to edit certain parts of the theme, such as the footer. I, personally, use Simple Edits (Figure 7.18). Once you install the plugin, you can access it under the Genesis folder on the left side of the Dashboard.

Installing Plugins You Download

If you decide to download a plugin instead of getting it directly from the WordPress Dashboard, please make certain it comes from a reputable programmer. You can easily bring security problems to your website with an out-of-date or even malicious plugin. Generally speaking, the only off-Dashboard plugins I install are pay versions of free plugins that are otherwise findable through the Dashboard.

To install a plugin from your computer, do the following (Steps 1–3 are shown in Figure 6.19):

Figure 6.19 Installing a Plugin from Your Computer

1. Access the Install Plugins page, as you would to install any other plugin.

2. Click on *Upload*.

3. Click on *Browse*.

4. Navigate to the file you downloaded and select it.

5. Click *Install Now*.

6. The rest of the steps are the same as for any other plugin.

Updating Plugins

It is crucial that you keep your plugins up-to-date. If you allow your plugins to become outdated, you could create security holes that hackers can use to infiltrate your site. In addition, you could lose functionality. Fortunately, WordPress lets you know when a plugin needs to be updated. You will see a number next to **Plugins** on the left side of your Dashboard. That number represents how many plugins need to be updated.

1. Click on *Plugins* and you will be brought to the Plugins page (see Figure 6.20a).

2. Click on *Update Available*. You will see a list of all plugins that can be updated.

3. Make sure the word **Update** appears in the top box as in Figure 6.20a.

4. Click the check box next to the plugin you want to update.

5. Click *Apply*.

Figure 6.20a Updating Plugins from the Dashboard

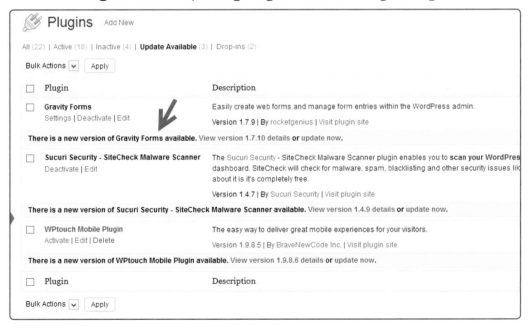

You can also update plugins on the Plugins page itself. You will see an alert that an update is available listed under any plugin that is out of date (see Figure 6.20b).

Figure 6.20b Updating Plugins from the Plugins Page

Deactivating and Uninstalling Plugins

It is very easy to deactivate or uninstall a plugin. Visit the Plugins page and click ***Deactivate*** to turn it off (see Figure 6.21). Once you deactivate a plugin, you can remove it entirely by clicking ***Delete*** (see Figure 6.22). You should delete inactivate plugins because they can become security holes. Keep in mind, if you remove a plugin that you rely upon, you could substantially alter the way your site works, so do not randomly deactivate and delete plugins unless you are sure you know what you are doing.

Figure 6.21 Deactivating a Plugin

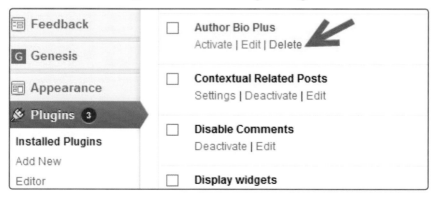

Figure 6.22 Deleting a Plugin

Conclusion

There are many plugins that will serve your site well. My recommendation is to stick with plugins that have at least a four-star rating. Begin with a small number of plugins and use only the ones that are actually necessary for your site. If you notice that your site slows down or has problems after you install a plugin, deactivate or remove the plugin and see if that resolves the problem. Do not use a plugin that has not been updated for several years. As mentioned, out-of-date plugins can cause serious security and functionality issues. Do not leave deactivated plugins on your site, since they can act as security holes. Delete them and reinstall them later if necessary.

Another helpful aspect of WordPress is that once you pick your theme, you can add a great deal of front-end functionality through tools called widgets. Widgets let you add menus for navigation, search boxes, links to your social media sites, and more. These powerful tools are addressed in Lesson 7.

Adding Functionality through Widgets

Widgets are items you can put on your website to add more functionality on the front end for users. This includes navigation tools, search boxes, links to social media sites, and more. Depending on your theme, some widgets might not be necessary or even usable with your website. A lot of widgets work in concert with plugins, which I addressed in Lesson 6.

Widgets in the Dashboard

To access widgets, click on *Appearance* and *Widgets*. You will then see the Widgets page (Figure 7.1), showing you what is already available for your site. As you add more plugins, additional options will appear.

How many widgets you can include on your site, and where you may place them, will be controlled by your theme. Some themes allow widgets on both sides and the bottom. Others limit widgets to only one side.

Figure 7.1 Widgets Page

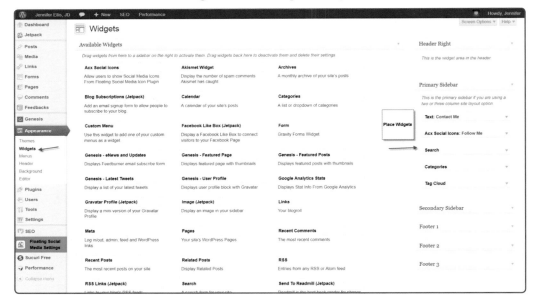

To work with a widget, you need only pick the one you want to use and then drag it to the appropriate widget area.

On my website, I use only a few widgets. They include a text box for contacts, a social media widget, a search box, categories (for blog posts), and a tag cloud (also for blog posts).

The text widget is especially useful. You can enter HTML code in this widget to provide links within your site or to other sites.

I recommend you keep the sidebar of your site relatively clean because it makes for easier navigation; so do not overdo it with the widgets. Just use whatever you need for appropriate functionality. If the theme you are using has widgets already sitting in the sidebar, you may remove them by simply dragging them out. You might want to put them in the box at the bottom of the page where inactive widgets are stored (see Figure 7.2). Then if you want to put them back you have easy access.

Use of Specific Widgets

There are several widgets you will most likely want to use, depending on whether they are already included in your theme.

Figure 7.2 Inactive Widgets Box

Navigation

Various themes have different ways of controlling navigation throughout your site. Proper navigation is critical because if people cannot easily move around your site and find the content, they will not stay. In some cases, you can create a menu,[37] but often you will use a simple text widget. A text widget is one that requires you to know a little bit of HTML, but fortunately, it is very simple.

For example, if I just want to include a simple e-mail contact and my phone number, I can do so with a text box, as in Figure 7.3.

Figure 7.3 Text Box Widget

---

37 See Lesson 8 for instructions on how to create a navigation menu.

Here, I placed an HTML e-mail link, which includes a subject line. The subject line tells me that people used the link from my website.

Similarly, I could set up simple text links for people to visit the different pages of my website. To add the code, I need to create an HTML link, which is as follows:

<a href="yourdomain.com/page.html">Link text</a>

I need to add a line telling the text box to put each of the links on its own line. To do that, I use the code <br> immediately after the code with the link. So, if I want a link to my home page in a text box, it would be:

<a href="jlellis.net/index.html">Home</a>

Next, I add as many of these as I would like to my text box, as shown in Figure 7.4:

Figure 7.4 Using a Text Widget for Simple Text Links

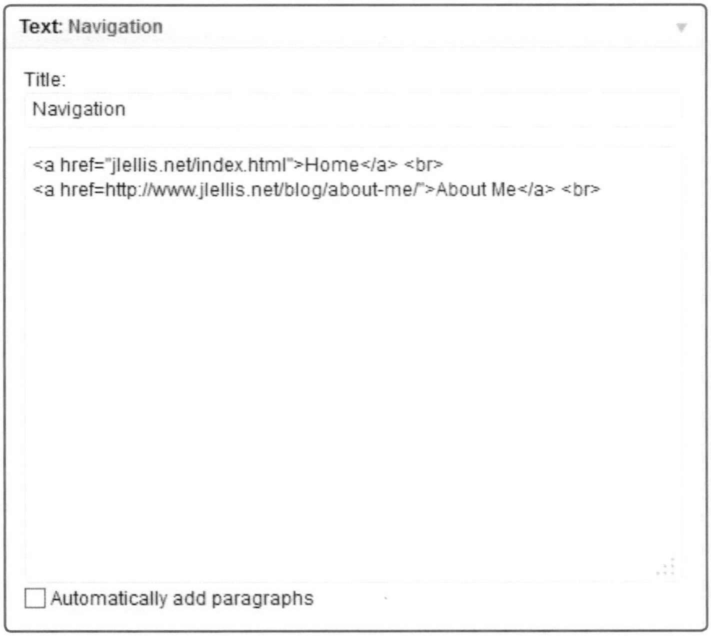

Text: Navigation

Title:
Navigation

<a href="jlellis.net/index.html">Home</a>
<a href=http://www.jlellis.net/blog/about-me/">About Me</a>

☐ Automatically add paragraphs

I click Save when I am done.

Once I do this, the widget on my website will look like the image shown in Figure 7.5:

Figure 7.5 Simple Text Links as Shown on Website

Search

Some themes include a search box, and some do not. It is very important to have a working search box somewhere on your website. Add one using the Search widget if your theme does not already have it.

If your website is not very robust in terms of pages, you might want the search box to show only on your blog and not on other pages. You can control where it appears by using the Display Widgets plugin I mentioned in Lesson 6.

To begin, simply click on the **_Search_** widget and drag it to the location where you would like the search box to appear.

As discussed in Lesson 6 on Plugins, the Display Widgets plugin controls what shows on different pages of my site. Figure 7.6 shows the back end of Display Widgets, where I choose which widgets show where. The result is shown in Figure 7.7, categories only show on my blog page, not on the other pages of my website. This keeps things looking cleaner for the regular content, where people don't need to see categories, but adds the information for blog content, where people would expect to see it.

Plugins and Widgets Together

If you recall from Lesson 6, I recommended a plugin called Acurax Social Icons that makes it easy to put links to your social media sites on your website. To use this plugin and widget, you first need to install the plugin as explained in Lesson 6.

Figure 7.6 Display Widgets Plugin

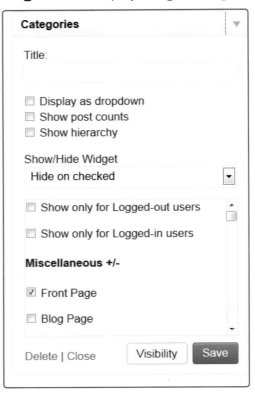

Figure 7.7 Showing Categories

Acurax will add two things to your website: (1) a sidebar item called **Floating Social Media Settings**, where you put in the links to each of your social media sites, and (2) a widget option that will appear in the Widgets page on your website (Figure 7.8). Fill in your links under **Floating Social Media Settings** (Figure 7.9) and then drag the widget to the part of your site where you want it to show. Figure 7.10 shows how the social media icons look on my website.

Figure 7.8

Figure 7.9 Acx Widget in Place

Figure 7.10 Social Media Icons on Website

Conclusion

Widgets are capable of adding a great deal of functionality to your website. Combined with plugins, that functionality is so great as to be staggering. The main thing to remember is that you want your website to be easy to read and navigate. If you overdo things, it will be confusing and difficult to use. Choose your widgets wisely. Ask others to look at your site, and then get their opinions on how easy or difficult it is to move around the pages and find your content.

Now your website is up and running. You have designed it to look the way you want. It is time to add content. I address how to do so in Lesson 8.

Adding Content

Now that the basic design of your website is ready, you can begin adding content. I explained how to add pages in Lesson 3, but let me refresh your memory.

Adding Pages

Here are the steps to follow on the Add New Page screen, which is shown in Figure 8.1.

1. Click *Pages*.
2. Click *Add New*.
3. An empty page will appear.
4. Enter the content.

Adding content to a WordPress page is very similar to adding content to a document in Word or any other program. Choose a title and put it in the title box. Then enter the content in the body of the page itself. Keep the title relatively short. The title will control the name of the link, but you can edit the link if you desire. You can also edit how the title will appear in Google for SEO purposes.[38]

5.   Click *Publish*.

Figure 8.1 Add New Page

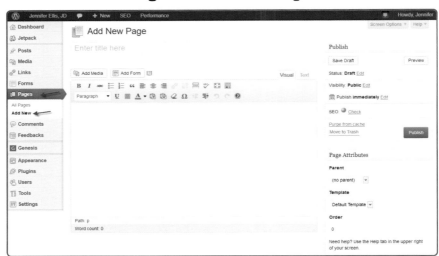

Formatting the Page

When you first begin working with WordPress, you will see a limited number of options for formatting on a page. You can fix this by clicking on the icon for WordPress's **Kitchen Sink** feature (see Figure 8.2). This will add more options, which are shown in Figure 8.3.

---

38 See Lesson 9.

Figure 8.2 Kitchen Sink Icon

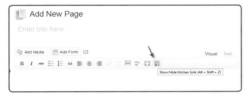

Figure 8.3 Kitchen Sink Options

Visual vs. Text

Generally speaking, you will be entering text on the visual screen. This is the screen that looks like any word processor. What you see in the visual screen is text with any images or formatting you have added, such as the screenshot in Figure 8.4.

Figure 8.4 Visual Screen

On occasion, you might feel the need to look at or work with the text version of page entry. This will allow you to actually see the code behind the page. Figure 8.4 and Figure 8.5 show the same exact page, but Figure 8.5 is the text version.

Figure 8.5 Text Version

Click on the ***Visual*** or ***Text*** tab to view the entry page in the version with which you desire to work. You will notice that the formatting options change depending on which tab you choose.

Adding Media

Click on ***Add Media*** (see Figure 8.6) to add images or other forms of media to a page or blog post.

Figure 8.6 Add Media

You will be taken to a page that allows you to add images or other forms of media by linking to or uploading the items. You can create a gallery of images on this page too. Also available is a media library composed of media you have uploaded in the past. You can click on a drop-down menu to see your options.

Uploading a Media File

Using images on web pages and blog posts is valuable both in terms of SEO and conversion rates. A good picture helps your audience understand, visually, what the page is about and can add an emotional connection for the viewer.

The following are the steps to upload a photo:

1. Click on ***Upload Files*** (see Figure 8.7).
2. Either drag the file to the noted location or click on ***Select Files***. If you click ***Select Files***, you will be able to browse through your files and upload your choice.
3. The file will be uploaded and will appear on the Insert Media page, shown in Figure 8.8.
4. Choose the alignment.
5. Choose the link. (You can link the photo to something else, so when people click on it, they will be taken to that link.)

Figure 8.7 Upload Files

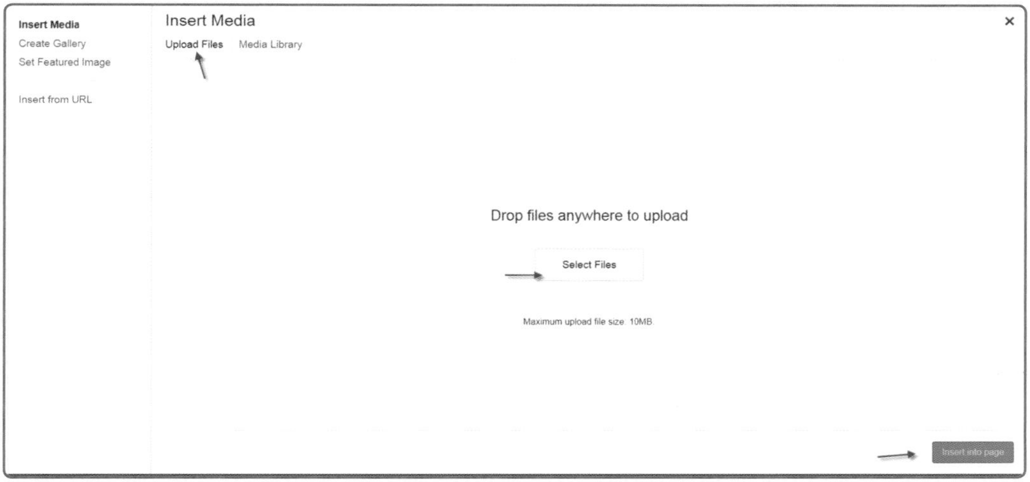

Figure 8.8 Insert Media Page

6. Choose a title.

   a. This helps you to easily search for images in the future.

7. Add a caption. (This is a notation that will appear under the photo.)

   a. If you do not want a caption, leave this blank.

Figure 8.9 Inserted Photo with Caption

8. **Alt Text** is text that appears when someone hovers a mouse over the photo.

   a. This is valuable for SEO. (See Lesson 9)

9. **Description** is a back-end description of the file.

10. Click ***Insert into page***. (Figure 8.9 shows a successfully inserted photo with a caption.)

Adding Media by Link

Adding a photo or other media file by link is much the same as uploading it.

1. Choose ***Insert from URL*** on the Add Media page (see Figure 8.10).

2. Paste the link in the box.

   a. If you are uncertain of the link to an image shown on another web page, right-click on it and choose ***Copy image URL***.[39] Then right-click and paste the link in the link location on your website. Please be sure that you have the right to use any image

---

39 The language for copying the URL will vary by browser. FireFox uses ***Copy Image Location***, for example.

you choose, and do not violate copyright by taking random images from the web or by searching Google.

Figure 8.10 Insert from URL Page

3. Once you paste the link, more options will appear (Figure 8.11), and you can complete them as appropriate.

Figure 8.11 Options for Adding Media by Link

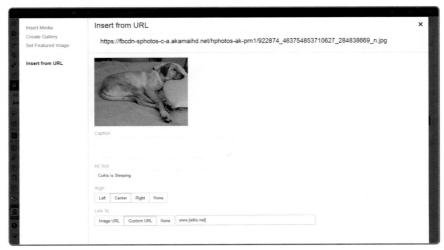

4. Add a caption (if desired).
5. Enter alternative text (**Alt Text**).
6. Choose the alignment.
7. Choose what you want to link the image to (if anything).
8. Click ***Insert into page***.
9. If the original image is too large, you will need to shrink it at this point.
   a. Click on the image to edit the size.

Resizing an Image

It is important to upload an image that is as close to the size you want to show as possible. If you upload an image that is too small, it will not look good. If you upload an image that is too large and shrink it using WordPress, the web page with the image will load more slowly as it resizes the image on the fly.[40] Regardless, you can either adjust the size of the image when you first insert it, or you can adjust it later on. There are three options:

1. Choose a percentage of the original size.
2. Choose the exact size under Advanced Settings.
3. Adjust the image by clicking and dragging on the image itself.

---

40 A popular plugin called Smush.it can be useful in avoiding the need to resize all images before you upload them. However, Smush.it can slow down uploading of images if the servers on which it is stored become too busy. In addition, very large images, as are common on most stock photo sites, can still cause problems for some websites and may be too large to upload at all as they are originally downloaded.

Changing Image Settings

Once an image is uploaded, you can make changes to its location, size, and several back-end items. To access the control panel, click on the image and click on the small square that looks like a nature scene (see Figure 8.12).

Figure 8.12 Accessing the Image Control Panel

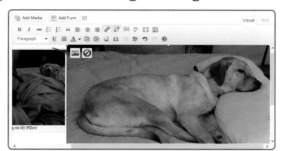

From here you can edit the title, change the alignment, and make several other basic adjustments, as shown in Figure 8.13.

Figure 8.13 Editing the Image

You will note that you can change the link of the image. The Link URL, accessed under the main edit box, allows you to make adjustments to the link connected to the image. When you first add an image it will either link to itself or the source from where you obtained it. Generally, I leave this blank. However, if you want an image to lead to a specific web page, for example a picture of a person to lead to a bio, this is where you would put the link.

You can also access more image options by clicking on the **Advanced Settings** tab.

In the Advanced Image Settings section, you can add a border or space around an image (see Figure 8.14). This will help you solve the problem of text bumping up against a photo. Enter a whole number in the appropriate box to add space or a border. The larger the number, the larger the space or the thicker the border.

Figure 8.14 Adding Space or a Border around an Image

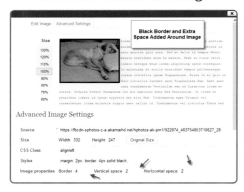

Changing the Link of a Page or Post

The link for every page is an important part of your SEO.[41] At the same time, you want to keep the links for your pages as short as possible. Depending on your permalink settings, the link will automatically match up with the title of the page, but you can change it by clicking on Edit next to the link (Figure 8.15). When you are finished, click OK (Figure 8.16).

---

41 See Lesson 9.

Figure 8.15 Editing a Link

Figure 8.16 Confirming an Edited Link

If you edit the link after you publish the page or blog post, you will change the location of the page. Anyone who has already linked to it will now have a broken link. Depending on how you link to items within your own site, you can cause broken links there too.

Editing Content

You can edit content on a page at any time (see Figure 8.17).

Figure 8.17 Editing Content on a Page

1. Click **Pages** in the Dashboard.

2. Click **All Pages**.

3. Find the page you want to edit and hover your mouse over it. An edit option will appear. Click **Edit**.

4. Edit the content.

5. Click **Update** when you are done.

Parent and Child Pages

On many websites, if you hover your mouse over a button, a list of other pages will appear. These pages are the "children" of the main, or "parent," page. For example, on my own site, I have About Me as a parent page. Underneath that I have one bio page for me and one for a staff member. When you hover your mouse over About Me, links for the two bio pages appear (see Figure 8.18). These two pages are the children of the About Me page. Even if you do not have a hover setup, organizing your site with parent and child pages is a good way to keep various topics together.

Figure 8.18 Parent and Child Pages

Creating a child page is done when you first create a new page or when you edit the page. The option is on the right side of the screen, in a drop-down list called **Parent** (see Figure 8.19).

When you open the drop-down list, you will see all of the other pages, as shown in Figure 8.20. Click the page you want to be the parent to the page you are currently editing. When you are finished, click Update (or Publish if you have not yet published the page).

Note: If you have published a page and later make it a child to another page, you will change the link. This means that if there are external links

Figure 8.19
Parent Page Attribute

to the page, those links might break, depending on your set up. It is best to set up parent/child relationships when you first create a page.

Figure 8.20
Drop-Down
Page List

Order of Pages in Menus

You can also control the order of how the pages appear in the menu on your website. This is done in a few ways.

Numbers

Figure 8.21
Ordering Pages
Using a Number

The first way to control the order of pages is by entering a number in a box on the page itself. On the right side of the page, under **Page Attributes**, is an **Order** box. Put the appropriate number in the box, as shown in Figure 8.21. This order will control both parent and child pages. In other words, if there are five main pages, the page with number 1 will appear first and the page with number 5 will appear last. If under parent page 1 there are five child pages, the child page with number 1 will appear first and the page with number 5 will appear last, underneath that parent page.

Plugins and Widgets

The next way to organize page order is through a widget or a plugin. There are numerous widgets that will serve this purpose. Two popular and well-reviewed plugins are Simple Page Order and Custom Page Order. There are many others that will serve the same purpose.[42]

---

42 See Lesson 7 for more on widgets.

Menus

The last way to order pages is to create a menu. Some themes allow menus; some do not. Some themes actively require menus. For example, the theme I use for my website will only allow me to have a navigation bar on my site through creating a menu. As a result, I used a menu to make the buttons across the top of my website. Following are the steps to create a menu for ordering pages.

Figure 8.22
First Steps to Create a Menu

1. Click on *Appearance*.
2. Click *Menus* (see Figure 8.22).
3. You will be taken to the Menus page (Figure 8.23, following the steps). At this point you will see if your theme supports menus and, if so, how many.
4. My theme allows for two menus, one on the top and one on the side. I just use the one on the side, which I call Main Navigation.

Figure 8.23 Menus Page

5. Under the **Main Navigation** tab, type a name for your menu in the box titled **Menu Name**. (Again, my menu is called Main Navigation.)

6. On the left side of the screen is a box called **Pages** with a list of your pages. Check the boxes for the pages you want to appear on your menu.

7. Click ***Add to Menu***.

8. You can also add categories to your menu. In the **Categories** box, choose the categories you want on your menu, and then click ***Add to Menu***.

9. Custom links are items that are not pages or categories—for example, an external site. If you want any of these items on your menu, go to the ***Custom Links*** box, type in the URL, provide a label, and click ***Add to Menu***.

10. Once you are done adding everything you want to show up on your menu, these items will appear underneath **Main Navigation** on the right side of the page.

11. Drag the labels into the proper order.

12. Indent child pages underneath parent pages. For example, as mentioned, About Me is a parent page. As you can see in Figure 8.23, Short Bio and About Beth are indented under About Me, so they show as child pages.

13. When finished, click ***Save Menu***.

You can edit your menu at any time. If you add new pages, you will need to adjust your menu accordingly. By checking **Automatically add new top-level pages** next to the Menu Name box (see Figure 8.23 above), you can set the site to automatically put any new parent pages on your menu. If you add too many top-level pages to your navigation bar on the top of your website, links will start to appear under each other.

Creating Blog Posts

Blog posts are created in a very similar way to web pages. The only difference is that instead of clicking on **Pages** on the Dashboard, you need to click on ***Posts***. Then click on ***Add New***. You will be taken to a blank post page (see Figure 8.24). Working with the post screen in terms of creating content is the same as working with the page screen.

Figure 8.24 Add New Post

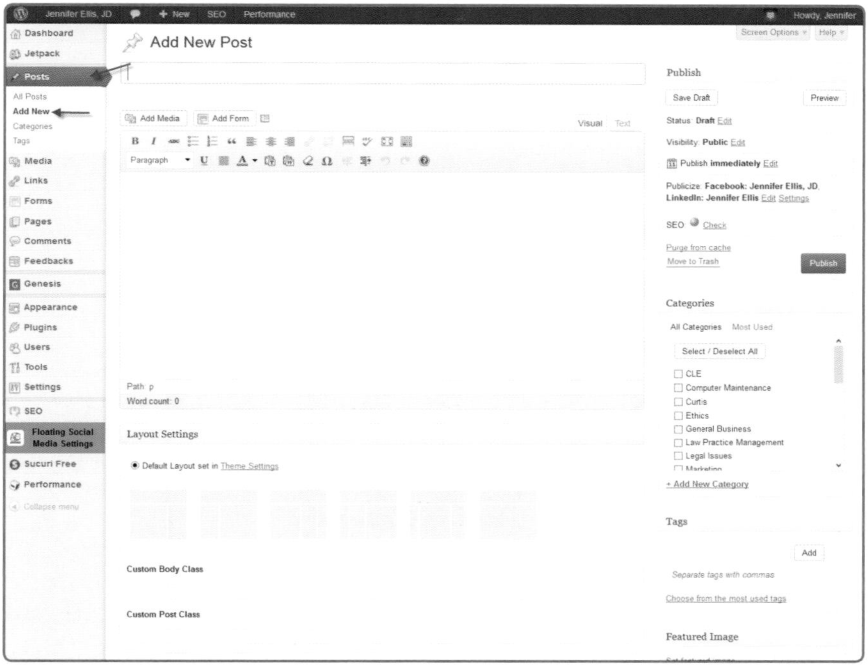

The differences between posts and pages amount to the ability to categorize and tag your posts.

Categories

Categories help people find content on your site. When you have a list of categories on your blog, if a user clicks on a category, he or she will be taken to a list of every post that fits within that category. Categories are helpful for SEO purposes as well.

Creating Categories

When you write your first post, you will see only one category, "Uncategorized." You will also see the option to add new categories on the post page. Type in the name for a category that you feel is appropriate for your post. As you post more and more, you will find yourself repeating categories, and over time, you will have a library of posts under each category. Once you have created a category, it will appear on a list; you only need create it once (see Figure 8.25). Check the box of the category (or categories) that is appropriate for your post. You can check as many categories per post as you want.

You can also place categories within categories; the main category is called the parent. When you create a new category, click on **Parent Category** (Figure 8.26) and you will see a list of your categories. Choose the one that fits as a good parent for your new category.

A category will show on your website only if you use the Categories option and widget, and have actually posted something under that category. Figure 8.27 shows an example of a list of categories on a web page.

Figure 8.25
Categories for Blog Posts

Figure 8.26
Parent Category

If you want to edit categories, you can do so from the Dashboard.

1. Click on ***Posts***.

2. Choose ***Categories***.

This will take you to a page listing all of your categories and information about those categories, as shown in Figure 8.28. If you hover your mouse over a category, you will see the option to edit or delete it.

Figure 8.27 List of Categories

Figure 8.28 Editing Categories

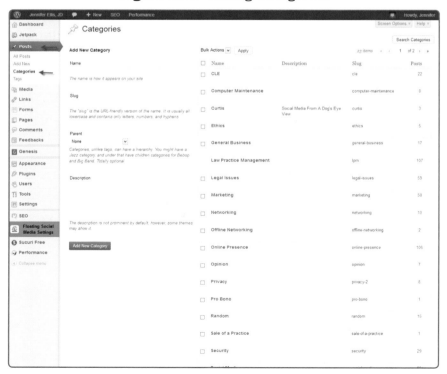

Tags

Tags are another way to help people navigate your site and are a useful SEO tool. Each post you write will have a focus, and the tags should point out that focus. For example, if you write a post about divorce and specifically address alimony and spousal support, you might make Divorce the category and tag the words alimony and spousal support. Put a comma between each tag. So in this case it would be alimony, spousal support. A list of tags is shown in Figure 8.29. If you want to see or reuse your previous tags, click on **Choose** from the most used tags.

You can use the Tag Cloud widget on your blog so people can see what you post about, click on the word or term that interests them, and be taken to the posts that have that word or term. Eventually, once you post enough, you will have a tag cloud, similar to the one shown in Figure 8.30. The cloud will have tags of different sizes. The larger the tag, the more frequently you have posted using that word or term. In order for the Cloud to actually work, you need to enter terms in the Tag field when you write posts.

Figure 8.29
Tag List

Figure 8.30
Tag Cloud

Editing Blog Posts

To edit a blog post, click **_Posts_** and **_All Posts_**. Hover over the post you want to edit and click **_Edit_** (see Figure 8.31). Click **_Update_** when you are finished.

Figure 8.31 Editing a Blog Post

Comments

As I have mentioned, I recommend you allow comments on your blog posts. Allowing comments increases the opportunity for communication, which in turn increases the likelihood that people will link to your posts. Links from other websites to yours increase your SEO.

You can control comment settings from the **Discussion** tab on the Dashboard, as noted in Lesson 3. Choose to moderate comments and you can prevent any negative or harmful comments from showing on your blog. If you install the Akismet plugin (see Lesson 7), common spam comments will be blocked and you will not have to deal with them.

Changing Time

A useful tool is the ability to post backward or forward in time (see Figure 8.32). Forward in time is helpful if you plan on being away for a while and would like to keep posting while you are gone. This feature is available for both pages and blog posts.

Figure 8.32 Changing Time of Publication

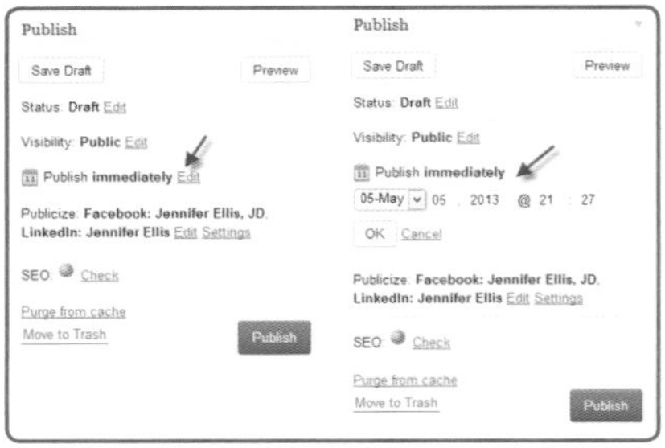

Conclusion

It is important to plan out your content and make certain it is high quality. Organize your site, using WordPress's tools, in a way that makes sense for the users. Include pictures to keep each page interesting. By doing so, you will be well on your way to a top notch website.

I cannot overstate the importance of high-quality content. The better the content, the more likely people will read it. Further, Google recognizes good content and as a result is more likely to give you a higher spot on its search engine. This is part of what we call SEO, and it is the next lesson in this book.

Search Engine Optimization

Search engine optimization (SEO) is a crucial part of your website. Essentially, your SEO dictates how easily people find your website when they are searching on Google, Bing, or Yahoo for topics related to your firm. SEO is complicated, but there are basic things you can do to give yourself a leg up on the competition. If you integrate some of these recommendations into your website efforts, you will have a solid start to your SEO.

Domain Name

I addressed the basics of choosing a domain name in Lesson 2. But as you go through the process of choosing your name, there are some SEO considerations to think about.

Exact-Match Domain Names

An **exact-match domain name** (EMD) might be something like divorcelaw.com or idahobusinesslaw.com. These domains can be very useful, since they include keywords people use in a search; however, they can also be damaging if used incorrectly. If you use an EMD, it is crucial that the content on the website be high quality. Otherwise Google's search algorithm will penalize the site.[43] Think about the keywords people would use to find your site and try to work them into a domain name. As with other domain names, it is frequently difficult to purchase the obvious keywords, and it might take some creativity to come up with an effective EMD for your firm. Be certain to run the appropriate checks, as mentioned in Lesson 2, to make sure the domain name you pick is acceptable.

I actually saw extensive harm done to the SEO of one law firm because it owned about 150 EMDs, all linking to its main site. Once we deactivated the names, the main site was able to recover a lot of its lost position on Google, but it took a little while.

More Than One Domain Name

Another old-school SEO tactic was to register a large number of domain names and have them lead to the same site. This is no longer effective. Do not register a lot of domain names. It will not help, and it will very likely hurt, your SEO. As I mentioned in Lesson 2 it is perfectly acceptable to use related versions of your domain name, such as different spellings that people are likely to type. For example, this can be very helpful if you have a commonly misspelled name. A couple of domain names is fine. But do not overdo it.

Website and Blog with Separate Domain Names

In the past, SEO folks always told their clients to use different domain names for the website and the blog. So, for example, in my case I might

---

43 Google implemented the EMD penalty in 2012. Essentially the goal is to prevent domain names that are exact matches to keywords from being successful simply because they have those keywords. If you are using an EMD, you do not need to get rid of it. What you need to do is make certain your site contains high-quality content.

have had my website on jlellis.com and my blog on jlellisblog.com. There is no particular reason to do this anymore, but if both sites have good content, there is no harm in doing so. Since you are most likely reading this book because you are in the process of creating your first website, you are best off just using one domain name for everything.

Organization

Google likes organization. It likes sites that make sense in terms of how it crawls[44] them. Visitors to your site also like organization. Make sure your pages are organized in a way that makes sense. Create a plan for your pages from the beginning, and it will help keep things neat.

Begin by thinking through what pages you want to have on your site. Typically, a law firm website will begin with certain pages. The titles will vary, but the purpose is pretty straightforward:

- **Home:** This is the page that welcomes users to your site. It should introduce you and your firm, show the areas of practice you offer, and give other basic information.
- **About:** This page will describe the firm in some detail. Normally the bio pages for the lawyers and staff will be children of this page.
- **Practice:** The various practice areas will usually be children of this parent page. Then there will be more children under each of the practice pages. This is often the most robust part of a law firm website.
- **Blog:** This will be the blog page.

---

44 The term crawl means that Google sends a program that is known as a web crawler, spider, or bot around the web to index web sites and web pages. When you search Google or any other search engine, you are not actually searching the web, you are searching the index.

- Contact and Disclaimer: You may or may not have these pages on the top menu of your site, but you should have a link to a disclaimer somewhere on your site. Some sites put the disclaimer information and contact form on the same page, while others keep them separate. I recommend that you have a contact form on every page of your site.[45]

There are numerous other types of pages you might have on your site. Think through what you want to convey and what information your potential clients will want to see. You can and should always be adding more pages. But you want your main parent pages to stay the same.

Child Pages

Child pages fall under parent pages.[46] It is important that your pages have a logical structure. For example, if you practice traffic law, you will have a practice area page listing specifically what you practice. Then, under that parent page, you will have each of the child pages: traffic tickets, DUI, and so on. Underneath each of those pages will be more pages; for example, you might put topics such as traffic signals and speeding under the traffic ticket page. The structure would be as follows:

1. Practice Areas
    a. Traffic Tickets
        i. Traffic Signals
        ii. Speeding
    b. DUI
2. About
    a. Why Hire Us

---

45 The Gravity Forms plugin is an excellent way to add a high-quality contact form. See Lesson 7.
46 See Lesson 8.

b. Lawyer Bios

c. Awards

d. Testimonials

Your site should continue on this way, with parent pages at the top and related child pages under each parent page as needed. You can have as many child pages under a parent page as appropriate. Think about the content you will want to write in the future. You can lay out the pages now and just save them as drafts. Don't publish them until you have completed the content.

Content, Content, Content

Nothing is more important than high-quality content for SEO. When you begin your website, you should write strong content that relates to your area of practice. That content should contain the appropriate keywords people are using to search for the information you are writing about. Nothing is better for helping people find your site than valuable, well-written content. As a result, when you write for a web page, your first focus should not be "this is how I create content for SEO" but "this is the best content for what I am trying to say."

What You Write

Write in plain English. Keep things short, straightforward, and to the point. That said, no page should be shorter than three hundred words. Each page should have a key purpose. For example, if you practice bankruptcy law, you will have a page on Chapter 7. The Chapter 7 page should focus on Chapter 7, and not on anything else.

Always have a call to action on your web pages, such as *Call us at 555-123-1212, E-mail us at [link], Contact us at [link].*

Once you write your content, go back and think about whether you have included the correct keywords. In time, you will start thinking about keywords while you are writing.

Keywords

People search the web in two ways. They input a series of words or they input a complete phrase or question. For example, someone might search "traffic ticket Harrisburg Pennsylvania" or "How can I beat a traffic ticket in Pennsylvania." In addition, people search by what are called short-tail and long-tail keywords. Short tail would be "traffic ticket," and long tail would be the phrase "How can I beat a traffic ticket in Pennsylvania."

You need to have content that meets these various types of searches. As you write, and when you review your first draft, think about how people search for help in the areas in which you practice. Then use those keywords and phrases in your writing. There are tools you can use to help identify keywords, such as Google's Keyword Planner.[47] Each page or blog post should focus on only one concept.

Remember, local search is very important. You are not just a family law attorney but also a family law lawyer. You are a Harrisburg, Pennsylvania, family law attorney. You are also a Harrisburg, Pennsylvania, family law lawyer. And a family law attorney in Harrisburg. The plural matters as well.

Recently, Google introduced its newest search algorithm, Hummingbird. This algorithm recognizes that people tend to run complicated searches as opposed to searches of just two or three words. As a result, if someone searches "How do I find a divorce lawyer in Phoenix" a blog post that has the title and/or phrase "How do I find a divorce lawyer" is much

---

47 https://support.google.com/adwords/answer/3141229

more likely to be successful than a page which simply attempts to focus on the keywords "Phoenix Divorce Lawyer." Especially if the first website is has high quality content, and ranks well in local search for Phoenix.

As you write, think about using both simple keywords "divorce lawyer" and more advanced phrases that match what people are seeking from you. You can often identify the right phrases by focusing on the questions clients ask you, and how they phrase those questions. Use the phrasing that the people actually use when you write your blog posts and pages. This is also an excellent source of ideas for posts. Please keep in mind that it is more important to have good content than to worry about getting each and every keyword into your page or blog post. Google does not like what is called "keyword stuffing," or overuse of the same keyword. As I mentioned already, the main point is to focus first on high-quality content that is readable and makes sense.

Titles

Titles matter. They should be short and succinct, as well as interesting. Fortunately, you can have an SEO title that is different from the actual title of your page. So while you might call your main page Home or Welcome or Index, the SEO title can be Chicago Divorce Attorney | Name of Firm. Include keywords in your title, but remember to balance functionality and SEO.

H1

There are various font sizes available from WordPress. Those sizes include Paragraph, which is what you will type most content in, but also H1, H2, H3, and so on. Google likes to see a strong H1 heading as the first piece of content within a page. Headings should include keywords. Use only one H1 heading on each page. You can use as many H2 or H3 headings as you like.

Changing the size of the font requires you to make sure you have turned on the Kitchen Sink feature (see Lesson 8) so you can see the various options (see Figure 9.1). Then you need to click in the box with the font size. The default is Paragraph.

Figure 9.1 Changing Font Size

Links

Links matter too. As with the title pages, links should be short. However, for SEO purposes, if they can contain a keyword or two, that is very valuable. The title you type on the top of the page or blog post will automatically become the link. You can edit the link to make it more appropriate, and you can remove words such as *and, of,* and *at* to shorten it. (See Lesson 8.)

Link to Other Content

A good website links not only to its own content but also to content on other sites. If you mention custody on your page about divorce, link to your custody page. If you write a blog post explaining some issue in custody, link the blog post to the custody page. Link to high-quality sites other than your own that will provide value to your users. Frequently link to your contact form or contact page.

Blog Posts

Blog posts can be about virtually anything, but obviously it is best if they relate to your practice. Blog posts are not briefs. They are informal pieces of writing, generally aimed at an eighth-grade level. Most lawyers write their blog posts as if they are writing to other lawyers. Unless your clients are other lawyers, this will not work and will turn potential clients off.

Here are some good ideas for blog posts:

- Answer questions people ask on the first consultation.
- Write about news stories related to your practice area(s).
- Analyze relevant cases.
- Talk about your life or what your firm is doing at whatever level you are comfortable.

It is important to keep your posts timely. If a topic is hot, write about it immediately. This will give you more visitors and a greatly increased likelihood that someone else will link to your post. The goal is for your content to be educational and compelling—hopefully, compelling enough that others will link to it. The more *quality* links you get to your site, the better your SEO.

Blog posts can and should have longer titles and links than pages. Posts should, when appropriate, link to reliable and helpful external content. A post should be at least three hundred words. The maximum length depends on your own style, but if it is too long, no one will read it.

Links to Your Site

You want to encourage links to your site. If quality websites link to yours, your profile on Google will increase. That said, you do not want to engage in link exchanges—that is, "give me a link on your site and I will give you a link on my site"— because Google penalizes this behavior. In addition, you want *high-quality* links. Quality over quantity is what matters here. The best way to get links to your site is to write good content that people want to link to because it is useful to their own readers.

Video

Video is very powerful content. There are various opinions on how good a camera you need to use and what kind of quality you need. My advice is to go ahead and get started with a decent cell phone camera. If you really get into video, you should invest in a good camera and a wireless lavaliere microphone. The camera I use for my firm is one we purchased for about $600. When you film, make sure you have an appropriate background and are in a quiet room. The air conditioner, for example, can be a lot louder than you realize. Having a wireless lavaliere will help with background noise.

You can upload your content to a variety of sites. (I generally use YouTube.) Then embed that content into your blog posts or pages. A video bio for each lawyer, paired with a written bio, can be a great way of introducing your lawyers to potential clients.

Embedding Video from YouTube to a Page or Post

To embed a video, you will need to get the embed code and paste it into the text entry portion of the page or post. This is one area where the visual screen will not work.

1. Upload the video to YouTube.
2. Go to the page for the video and click on **Share** (see Figure 9.2).

Figure 9.2 Getting Your Uploaded Video from YouTube

3. Click on *Embed* (see Figure 9.3).

4. Make sure *Show suggested videos when the video finishes* is unchecked.

5. Copy the embed code.

Figure 9.3 Embedding a YouTube Video

6. Go to the page or post where you would like to embed the video.

7. Choose *Text* (instead of **Visual**) for entering content (see Figure 9.4).

8. Paste the embed code where you would like the video.

Figure 9.4 Add New Post (Embed Video)

9. Publish or update the page and make sure the video works. A sample page with embedded video is shown in Figure 9.5.

Figure 9.5 Sample Page with Embedded Video

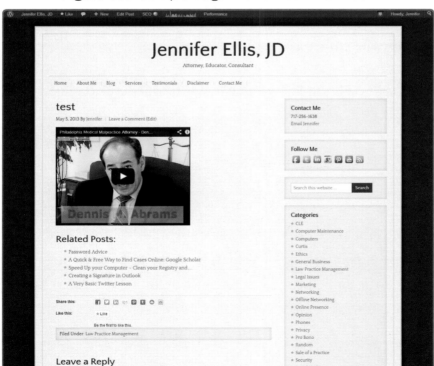

Use Pictures

People are drawn to pictures, and good pictures can encourage someone to read your web page or blog post. Be sure to give your pictures appropriate titles for SEO. Pictures are fine on both pages and posts, but do not use typical stock photos. Avoid gavels, scales, pictures of courthouses, and so on. These are boring and overused. Try to find pictures that relate to your practice or to what you are writing about.

To give a picture the appropriate SEO, you need to change what is called the alt text. Do this when you first upload the picture. You will see a box labeled **Alternative Text** (see Lesson 8). Enter the information about the picture in this box. Be sure you use the keywords you want to feature.[48]

For example, if you represent DUI clients in Phoenix and are writing a page on DUI law, your key words will likely be something along the lines of Phoenix DUI Attorney. The alt text on a picture for the page should be Phoenix DUI Attorney. You can also include the name of your firm, in which case the alt text would be Phoenix DUI Attorney – XYZ & Associates, LLC.

WordPress SEO by Yoast

I recommended the WordPress SEO plugin in Lesson 7 because it is, in my experience, the best SEO tool for WordPress. This plugin helps you determine whether you have the appropriate SEO. It offers suggestions if your SEO is not up to snuff. It will even warn you if you have used a keyword too few or too many times.

If you install the WordPress SEO plugin, when you create a new post or page (or edit one), you will see the SEO panel on the bottom of the page. When you write your content, decide on a keyword or phrase and then enter it in the *Focus* box. Once you enter this term, WordPress SEO

---

48 If you need to add alternative text after you have already uploaded an image, see Lesson 8.

will look for it in the appropriate locations.

A color code will inform you how well you have done. Green is for very good; red is for very bad (see Figure 9.6). Gray indicates that you did not enter a focus term.

To find out specifically what you can fix, click on the **_Page Analysis_** tab (see Figure 9.7). You will see a series of color-coded notes

Figure 9.6 Focus Keyword Status

informing you what you have done well and what needs to be improved. As you make adjustments, you will see the items change, and if you did not have a green SEO result for your focus term, you will see the color change as you improve the SEO on the page or post.

Figure 9.7 Page Analysis

Social Media

Social media is an extremely important part of SEO. If you are not cur-rently using social media to market your firm, it is time to start doing so. A detailed lesson on social media is outside the scope of this book, but the ABA has a number of excellent resources on LinkedIn, Facebook, and Twitter. (You also should be using Google+.)

Your goal should be to use social media both as a networking tool and as a place to share the blog posts you write for your website. On some sites you can share the picture you used in your post, the title of the post, and a bit of information about what you covered. Then you simply add the link. On Twitter, since you only have 140 characters, you will need to be more selective in what you share. The goal is to get as many people to see the post as possible.

Conclusion

If all of this information seems like too much to you, don't worry. Focus first on your content. Write high-quality, informative, easy-to-understand pages and posts. If you do so, Google will reward you.

The market in which you find yourself will have a big impact on how much you have to worry about your SEO. If you are in a small market and practicing in a niche area, you won't have to worry too much. If you are in New York City and practicing bankruptcy law, you might need to consider retaining help due to the extremely competitive nature of the market and the difficulty you will have in getting to the first page on Google.

As lawyers, it is crucial to remember that we cannot create a website and content in a vacuum. We have ethical obligations we absolutely must follow. I have left what can be considered the most important issue for the last lesson: ethics.

Ethics

Ethics are a very important part of websites and blogging. If you do not follow the ethical rules, you could find yourself on the wrong side of a complaint. Fortunately, there have not been too many instances of lawyers getting into trouble due to their blogs, but there are a few. In the end, common sense is mainly what you will need to avoid problems. Just remember not to do anything online that you can't or wouldn't do off-line, and you should be OK. Also, familiarize yourself with the ethical rules involving marketing in your jurisdiction(s).

Websites Are Considered Law Firm Advertising

There is no doubt that websites are marketing. Therefore, you must follow the ABA's Model Rules pertaining to marketing and advertising and/or the rules as adopted in your jurisdiction. Following are some specific rules that impact lawyers in Pennsylvania. Please check your own jurisdiction's rules, and keep in mind that a firm must follow all rules for all of the jurisdictions in which any of its lawyers are licensed.

Honesty

The overarching issue surrounding ethical rules generally and for marketing is that all communications must be honest. Therefore, nothing on your site should be false or misleading.

For example, if you state on your site that there is no fee if there is no recovery, that means there can be no litigation fees, court costs, or any other fees charged to your client if you do not recover money for the client.[49]

Expectations

Be careful not to suggest outcomes or create expectations by listing previous cases and verdicts or settlements. It is acceptable to do so *in some states*, but you must include a disclaimer, and sometimes very specific wording is required. For example, New York requires the statement "Prior results do not guarantee a similar outcome."

Domain Names

Do not pick a domain name that implies you are something other than what you are. For example, if you are a solo, your domain name should not suggest there is more than one lawyer in your firm. Thus, the domain name abcattorneys.com would not be acceptable, but abcattorney.com would be fine.

Office Name

Do not use the term "offices of" if you do not have more than one office.

---

49 *Zauderer v. Office of Disciplinary Counsel*, 471 U.S. 626 (1985). This case dealt with printed advertising but is used by disciplinary counsel for websites as well.

Specialist and Expert

Many states have very specific requirements about who may be listed as a specialist or an expert. Make sure you know and obey the rules in your jurisdiction(s). In Pennsylvania, you can only call yourself a specialist if you practice in certain areas or have passed a test approved by the Supreme Court of Pennsylvania.

Comments, Communication, and Unauthorized Practice

While I encourage use of comments on blogs,[50] it is very important to beware of forming a lawyer-client relationship with someone by answering legal questions in too specific a manner. Further, you could end up answering a question in a state where you are not licensed to practice, since the person asking the question could be from anywhere. If someone asks a legal question in a comment, it is best to have the person call you privately if you are in the same state or to send the person to another lawyer or a bar referral service if you are not in the same state. Be cautious.

Disclaimer

It is crucial that you have an appropriate disclaimer on every page of your site. In addition, you should have a more detailed disclaimer page, linked to the mini-disclaimers. What should these disclaimers contain? Well, that will vary by jurisdiction.

---

50 See Lesson 8.

The mini-disclaimer (that appears on every page)[51] should include (at least)

- a statement that the content is informational and is not legal advice,
- a clear notice that using the site is not forming a lawyer-client relationship, and
- a suggestion to read the full disclaimer, with a link to that page.

The full disclaimer should add (at least)

- jurisdictional limitations,
- confidentiality concerns (i.e., care in what is submitted and how it is sent),
- information addressing any awards or other items listed on the site, and
- everything in the mini-disclaimer, with more details.

If you plan on discussing cases, either in a blog post or somewhere on your site, you need to take several steps, including the following:

- Include a disclaimer *on the post or page* making it clear that past results do not guarantee future results.
- Protect your clients' confidentiality.

If you plan on using testimonials, be sure to address these issues:

- Make sure the testimonials in and of themselves are ethical.
  - In Pennsylvania, for example, you may not have an endorsement from a famous person.

---

51 If you cannot add a disclaimer to the bottom of the site due to limitations in your theme, you can put it elsewhere. This is also one time when I do recommended altering code. I provide instructions on how to do so in Appendix B.

- In most states, you cannot have certain kinds of language suggesting definite results.
- Do not compensate anyone for testimonials.

If you plan on using a contact form (and you should), here are two recommendations:

- Be very clear about confidentiality concerns.
- Consider having a box users must check to acknowledge they have read your disclaimer.

Blogs

There is disagreement as to whether blogs are marketing. In my view, the simplest way to avoid the problem is to include an appropriate disclaimer on your blog, regardless. If your blog is part of your website, you will have the same disclaimer there automatically. If the blog is a separate site, even if it's linked to your website, you will need to add a disclaimer. The disclaimer should be much the same as for your website. In addition, consider the following issues:

- If you are allowing comments on your blog, make it clear that people should not provide confidential information in the comments.
- If someone asks for advice, be careful how you answer the question. Do not provide legal advice on your blog. Offer general information and then direct the questioner to call you, or send the person elsewhere for assistance.

- Keep your blog posts general. Do not provide specific legal advice; that is, do not give instructions such as "do this, do not do that, or the result will be" in your posts.

Back Up Your Site and Keep Copies

Keep a copy of your site. Some states require you to keep copies of your site for a certain period of time; in Pennsylvania it is two years. The easiest way to do this is to back up your site and keep copies. You can also use software that will periodically download your site.

There are a variety of ways to back up your site. One way is to export the content. Another is to use a host, such as Bluehost, that includes automatic backup. Still another is to purchase the VaultPress backup that works with the Jetpack plugin.[52] This costs $20 per month. You also can make a backup of your site by downloading a copy of all of the files using your FTP software.

Of course, you do not want to back up your site only for ethics reasons. If you do not have a backup and something goes wrong, you will not be very happy. The export backup does not keep anything but the content of your site. It does not preserve your theme. The best backup to use is an external one that backs up both the content and the design.

> **HOW TO EXPORT YOUR CONTENT**
>
> 1. Click on **Tools**.
> 2. Click on **Export**.
>   a. If Export is not available, go to **Plugins**, search for Export, and install it. Then return to step 2.
> 3. Make sure **All Content** is selected.
> 4. Click Download Export File.

---

52 See Lesson 6.

Security

Due to ethical reasons, for the safety of your site and the safety of your site's users, it is important that you practice good security. Because Word-Press is popular, hackers frequently try to break into WordPress sites. They do this for a variety of reasons. Sometimes they are just malicious and want to spread malware. More frequently, they want to insert malware into your site that will somehow benefit them financially. You might wonder why security relates to ethics. It is because certain kinds of malware, if put into your site, can then be downloaded to your firm or to your clients and steal data from their computers. Fortunately, there are steps you can take to keep your site and users safe.

Keep Your Site Up-to-Date

If not kept up-to-date, WordPress itself, along with plugins and themes, can become a security hole. Always update anything that needs updating. Get in the habit of checking the Dashboard at least once a week to see if there are any updates. WordPress will tell you if it needs to be updated or if any plugins need to be updated. It will also tell you if a theme has an update, if that theme is a WordPress theme or was installed through Genesis or a similar product. Only purchase a theme from someone who keeps it up-to-date and provides you with the updates.

Choose Safe Plugins, Themes, and Widgets

Use only current plugins. I have mentioned already that you should not use a plugin that has not been updated for a long time. This is because such an item could have security holes, leaving your site open to malware attacks. Only use items that are obtained from the WordPress Dashboard and have high ratings, or that are from well-known and respected WordPress coders. If you are not sure, use Google to research the item you plan on installing.

Use a Scanner

There are a variety of services you can install to work with your site that will constantly scan it for malware. If your site becomes infected, the service will automatically remove the malware (if it can) and/or report the problem to you. The service includes manual removal of malware if the service cannot automatically remove it (or if automatic removal is not offered). I use Sucuri[53] for my websites. I have even used it to clean a site that got infected. The service comes with a plugin and will send you texts if something attacks your site. As mentioned previously, Sucuri comes with the web host Synthesis for free.

Conclusion

Remember, a website is marketing and therefore must be treated as such. All ethical rules must be followed. Further, WordPress, because it is so popular, is often under attack by hackers who seek to infect sites with malware or steal data. As a result, you must be certain to keep your site up-to-date and secure.

---

53 http://sucuri.net/

Conclusion

Every law firm should have a website. Regardless of your skill set, you can create your own WordPress-based site and have a finished product you are proud to share with potential clients. Take advantage of WordPress and the many tools you can use to increase its functionality. Begin slowly, and build your site over time. There is no need to rush the final process. But there is a need these days to have at least a basic website up and running as soon as possible. I hope you found this book useful in helping you navigate how to create your own website using WordPress.

My Hosting Experiences

I have used a few different hosts over the past several years, and I am going to share my experiences with you so you can learn from my mistakes. If you do have a problem with your host, it is certainly possible to change. In fact, if you are unhappy with your host early on, change it as soon as you can. However, changing hosts does add a level of complexity it is best to avoid, so try to pick a good host in the beginning.

GoDaddy

The first host I used was GoDaddy, and it turned out to be a disaster. I started with a five-page HTML site, for which GoDaddy was fine. However, when I switched to WordPress, my site was consistently slow and even timing out. Timing out means when people tried to access the site they received an error message. I repeatedly contacted GoDaddy, only to be informed that there was nothing wrong on its end.

I tried every bit of troubleshooting required, but in the end I decided that GoDaddy was simply not the place to have a WordPress site. Sure enough, when I moved my site, the problems stopped. In addition, GoDaddy had a pretty famous outage in 2012 that caused a lot of trouble for many people. I can safely say it is the last web host I would recommend. (Incidentally, this feeling is not based on the arguably offensive commercials for which GoDaddy is so famous, but those ads do not help.) I do, however, think GoDaddy is very good for registering domain names.

1&1

The second host, which I still use, is 1&1. 1&1 is an excellent web host, with the exception of two things. First, it does not have a one-click option for installation of WordPress. I do not believe the average lawyer will want to install WordPress manually.

Second, it limits some of the settings you are able to control. This means that I routinely have problems getting 1&1 to play well with such things as Office 365, the cloud system I use and recommend for e-mail. I have spent entirely too many hours on the phone with technical support for both Microsoft and 1&1 for things that would be easy if 1&1 simply allowed the kinds of settings that other web hosts generally allow. Understand, tech support always tried to be helpful and was good with many problems, but I prefer to avoid the phone calls in the first place.

As a result, while I manage many websites on 1&1 and rarely experience problems with the sites themselves, I do not recommend it as a host for most people. There are simply too many issues that can arise for an inexperienced person who wants to manage his or her own site.

Rackspace

I used the Rackspace service for about two months. I started using it once we took on managing the hosting of my law firm's website on our own. Rackspace features a cloud-based service that provides one-click WordPress installation. The combination of Rackspace's reputation and this service for WordPress led me to choose it, and I had high hopes. Unfortunately, I ended up very disappointed. The speed of the website was extremely slow; so much so that I wondered if there was something wrong with the site itself. But as soon as I moved the site to the host we use now, it was blazing fast, so the problem was the host, not the site. Frankly, given Rackspace's reputation, I was quite surprised at what happened. Given my experience and the fact that Rackspace charges $150 per month for cloud-based WordPress hosting, I cannot recommend it.

Bluehost

The current host for my own WordPress-based site is Bluehost. It has the one-click WordPress installation I like to see, and it allows full control of the various aspects of the domains. However, I have experienced two problems. The first is that many Bluehost sites went down for several hours in 2012. This happens with many of the lower-cost hosts, unfortunately. Second, sometimes I find Bluehost's cPanel (otherwise known as the control panel) to be a bit confusing and slow. However, technical support is very helpful, and I have otherwise been very happy with this service. Therefore, based on my own experiences as well as its consistently high reviews, I am happy to recommend Bluehost.

HostGator

HostGator is much like Bluehost. It has the one-click WordPress install, is highly rated, and is easy to use. My law firm previously had its site on HostGator and I had no problems. The control panel is straightforward enough, and the technical support is excellent. However, HostGator experienced its own outage in 2012. That said, due to my overall experience and the general reviews of the service, I feel safe in recommending it as a host. I have never experienced a crash on it. HostGator is also where my firm's former web designer kept our sites.

Synthesis

Synthesis is where I host my law firm's website now. I made the move at the end of August 2013, so my experience with the service is still quite new at the time this book is being written. The installation is easy because WordPress is already installed when you begin. Moving the site from Rackspace to Synthesis was straightforward. Synthesis does have some limitations in that it discourages the use of certain plugins.[54] But it does so because of difficulties with them. At this point, I am optimistic and feel that Synthesis is a good host to use for WordPress sites.

Conclusion

There are numerous hosting options from which to choose. My recommendation is that you do some research, look for the top-ranked hosts, and seek out reviews from people who have had positive and negative experiences. Then make your choice.

---

54 See Lesson 6 for information on plugins.

Instructions If the Host Does Not Offer One-Click Installation

Someone who has installed WordPress previously should be able to do this quite quickly, so if you decide to hire someone to do the install, it should not take more than thirty to sixty minutes, unless you have a host that complicates matters.

Preparation for the Installation

Make sure you have the following:

1. Access to your web server. In other words, you need to be able to log in to your web host and access where your website will be stored. For example, if you have chosen 1&1 as your host, you will need your username and password.

2. An FTP (File Transfer Protocol) client. I recommend Cute FTP[55] or FileZilla[56] for their ease of use. Some hosts have an internal FTP system that will allow you to upload files without needing an external client.

---

55 http://www.cuteftp.com/
56 https://filezilla-project.org/download.php?type=client

3. A web browser. For example, Internet Explorer, Firefox, Chrome, and Safari.

Installation

There are several steps to setting up WordPress on your own.[57]

1. Creating a database
2. Downloading the software
3. Uploading the software
4. Running the script

If step 4 does not work properly, it is because something went wrong with a previous step or your web host is not being cooperative.

Step 1: Creating a Database

One of the reasons WordPress is such a great tool is that it runs using a database. Well-coded databases keep things nicely organized and are easy to update. However, to properly install WordPress, you need to actually create a database before you upload the files. How you create the database will vary based upon your host. The most common tools used by hosts are called **MySQL**, **cPanel**, and **phpMyAdmin**.

MySQL

1. Log in to your web host.
2. Access MySQL.

---

57 Detailed instructions for the "Famous 5-Minute Install" are available online at http://codex.wordpress.org/ Installing_WordPress. A portion of the instructions provided in this book are copied or paraphrased from the linked directions, which are consistently kept up-to-date and are always a good place to look if you run into any problems.

3. Click on ***New Database***.

4. Enter a name for the database and choose a password. Make sure the password is strong. It should be a combination of letters (uppercase and lowercase), numbers, and symbols. It is best to pick at least ten characters. Be sure you write down the password, for now, so you can use it again later. When you are ready, click ***Set Up***.

5. You will be taken to a page containing details about the database. *Make sure you print this page so you have the information.* You will need it. Normally it will take a few minutes for the setup of the database to be completed, so be patient. In the meantime, click ***Go to Overview*** to return to the database page.

6. When the database is ready, you will see a notation next to it on the database page with the word **Ready**.

cPanel

cPanel[58] has a tool called the **Database Wizard**, which you will use to create a new database.

1. Access ***cPanel*** on your host.

2. Access the ***Database Wizard***.

3. Click ***Create a Database***.

    a. In the empty **New Database** field, type a name (e.g., Website, Blog, whatever works for you).

    b. Click ***Create Database*** (or ***Next***).

4. Create the database user.[59]

    a. Locate the **Username** field.

---

58 Directions on installing WordPress with cPanel can be found at http://docs.cpanel.net/twiki/bin/view/All-Documentation/CpanelDocs/Wordpress.

59 In some cases, it is not necessary to create a user. If you do not see this option, it is likely your cPanel does not require creation of a user.

b. Enter a name for the user.

c. Enter a password (pick a very strong password: at least ten characters with upper- and lowercase letters, numbers, and symbols).

d. Click **Create User**.

5. Click **Submit**.

6. You will be sent to a page with several options.

7. Complete the process.

a. *Write down* the host name, database name, username, and password. The host name is normally **localhost**.

phpMyAdmin

1. First, check to see if a WordPress database already exists. If not, follow the steps to create one.

2. Look on the left of the screen, and you will see a drop-down for **Database**.

a. Click on **Create Database**.

b. Put a name in **Create New Database**.

c. Click **Create**.

3. Click the **Home** icon on the upper left.

4. Click **Privileges**.

5. If no user for WordPress already exists, create one.

a. Click **Add a new user**.

b. Put a name in the **User name** field.

c. Choose a strong password (ten characters at least: uppercase and lowercase letters, numbers, and symbols).

d. Leave **Global Privileges** as they are.

e. Click **Go**.

6. Go back to **Privileges**.
   a. Click ***Check Privileges***.
   b. Access ***Database-specific privileges***.
   c. Select the database you created.
   d. Click ***Add Privileges on the following database*** (a drop-down).
   e. Click ***Check All***.
   f. Click ***Go***.
7. *Write down all the details*, including database name, username, password, and host name. The host name is normally **localhost**.

Step 2: Download the Software

1. Download the most recent version of WordPress. The most recent version can always be found at http://wordpress.org/download/. You should see a screen similar to the one in Figure B.1.

Figure B.1 WordPress Download Screen

2. Unzip the file to your hard drive. I generally suggest creating a folder on your desktop and putting the files in that folder so you can easily find them. If you do not have

software that allows for unzipping, you can download WinZip.[60] On my computer, I can extract (or unzip) a file by right-clicking and choosing **Extract**. For WordPress, the command would appear as shown in Figure B.2.

Figure B.2
Extract (Unzip)
WordPress

Once you click on **Extract** or **Unzip**, depending on your software, you will see a folder that contains all of the WordPress files. Be certain you extract the files to somewhere you can find them. This will be a folder with the name you gave it (in my case, word-press-3.5.2), which when opened shows all of the WordPress files. These are the files that you will need to upload to your web server (Figure B.3).

Figure B.3 WordPress Files

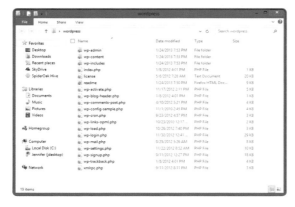

3. Upload the WordPress files.

---

60 WinZip is available for Windows or Mac at http://www.winzip.com/win/en/index.htm.

Where you upload the files will depend on how you want your website to be accessed. Since this book is about creating an entire website from WordPress, you will most likely want to install all the files to the main directory, so you would install them on what is called the root of your domain. In my case, that would be http://jlellis.com. If you prefer a sub-directory, create a new folder using your FTP software and then install WordPress to that subdirectory. For example, if I wanted to use a subdirectory, I would create the folder /blog/ and then install WordPress to http://jlellis.com/blog.

You can upload the files in one of two ways: use an external FTP program, or use a tool contained within the server. The choice will depend on your host.

If you need to use an external FTP program, you must have an FTP account to upload the software. Setting up the account will vary by host.

Open your FTP client and set it up using the FTP point for your site, which will most likely be ftp.yourdomain.com, and the username and password you created when you made your FTP account. Most FTP programs look the same once you are connected. The files on the left are those on your own computer, and the files on the right are those on the server.

Begin on the right side. Navigate your way to the location of the WordPress files on your hard drive. Then, looking at the left side, make certain you are on the correct directory in the server. If you will be uploading your files to the root directory, you should already be in the right place. Select all of the WordPress files and upload them to your server (Figure B.4). There are a lot of files, so they will take awhile to upload, depending on the speed of your Internet connection and your server.

Figure B.4
Uploading WordPress
Files to Server

Once all of the files are uploaded, they should appear on both the left and right sides (see Figure B.5).

Figure B.5 Successful WordPress Upload

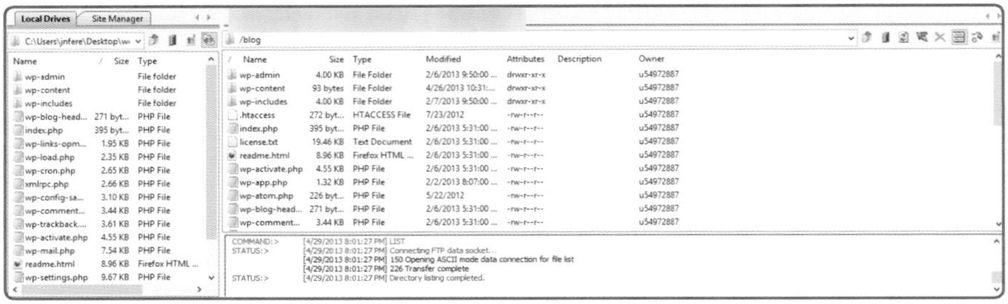

4. Run the script.

Once you have uploaded the files, you will run the installation script through your web browser. The script will run from wherever you uploaded the files (either your root directory or your subdirectory).

If you uploaded the files to the root directory, simply go to http://domain.com/wp-admin/install.php, and you will see the option to run the script. If you uploaded the files to a blog subdirectory, go to the subdirectory; for example, http://domain.com/blog/wp-admin/install.php.

Once you begin running the script, you should see a welcome page, as shown in Figure B.6.[61] Click *Let's go!* to set up WordPress.

---

61 If you receive a 404 or other kind of "page cannot be found" error, something went wrong with your download or upload. Make sure that you followed the steps properly. If you think you did everything right, contact your host's technical support for assistance.

Figure B.6 WordPress Welcome Page

At this point, one of two things will happen. You will see a message warning you that wp-config.php cannot be found and suggesting that you create it manually (Figure B.7), or you will see a page requiring some information from you. In either case, this is the point at which you will need the information I told you to save.

Figure B.7 Missing wp-config.php File

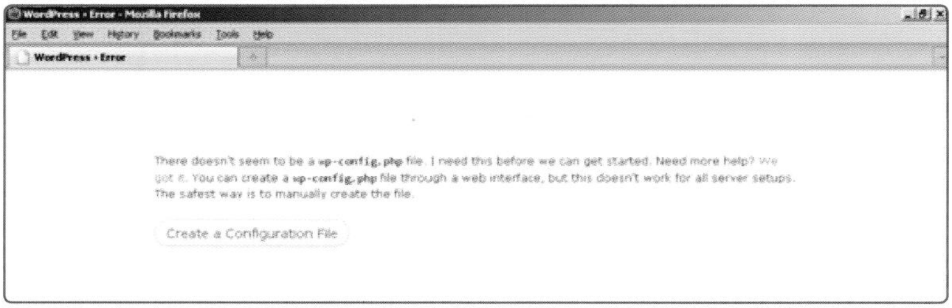

Continue through the pages until you see the page requesting the information you saved. Enter the data in the appropriate boxes (see Figure B.8). It is crucial that you enter each item correctly, or the script will not work. Note: In most cases, **localhost** is the name for Database Host. This is not the case with some hosts, such as 1&1, that provide specific database names, so make certain you have the correct information.

Figure B.8 WordPress Setup Page

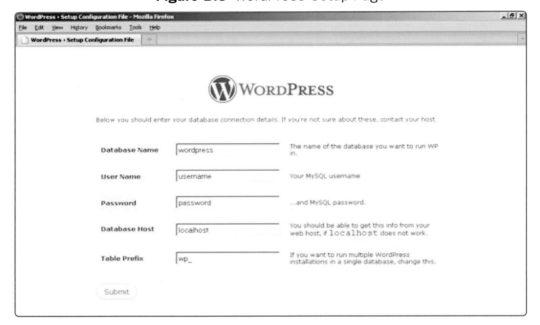

Problem with the Config File

A common error people run into is that WordPress is unable to create what is called the **config file**. If this happens to you, first make sure you entered the database name, username, and password correctly. If you have entered the correct information, the issue is one involving permissions, meaning that the script does not have the access it needs to create the file.

Fortunately, there is a way around the problem.

Go back to the WordPress files stored on your computer, and find the wp-config-sample.php file. (Figure B.9)

Figure B.9 Locating the wp-config-sample.php File

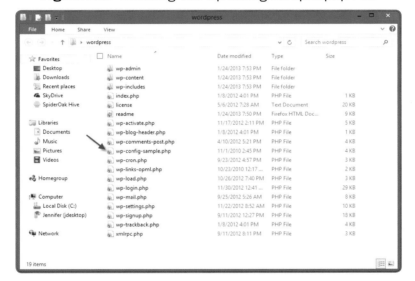

Once you open the file, you will see what is located in Figure B.10, except it will be longer (and will not have the highlighted text). Enter the appropriate information in each of the highlighted fields.

Figure B.10 Editing the wp-config-sample.php File

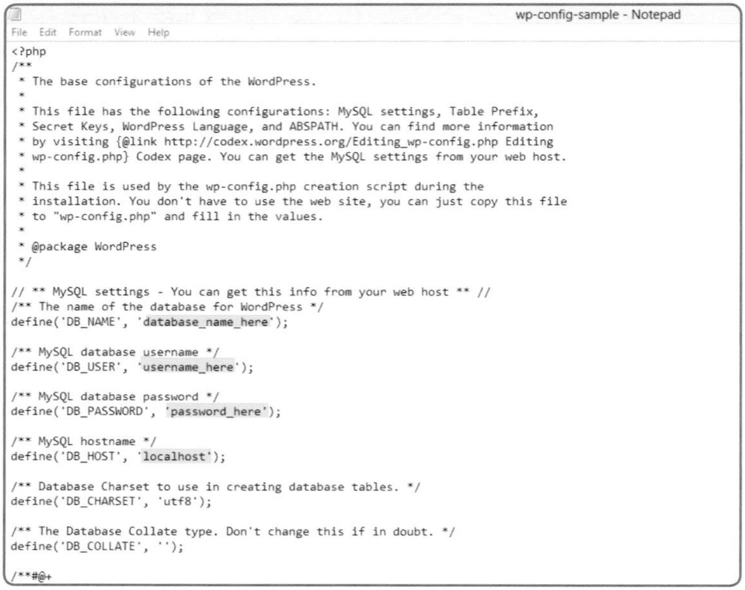


```
<?php
/**
 * The base configurations of the WordPress.
 *
 * This file has the following configurations: MySQL settings, Table Prefix,
 * Secret Keys, WordPress Language, and ABSPATH. You can find more information
 * by visiting {@link http://codex.wordpress.org/Editing_wp-config.php Editing
 * wp-config.php} Codex page. You can get the MySQL settings from your web host.
 *
 * This file is used by the wp-config.php creation script during the
 * installation. You don't have to use the web site, you can just copy this file
 * to "wp-config.php" and fill in the values.
 *
 * @package WordPress
 */

// ** MySQL settings - You can get this info from your web host ** //
/** The name of the database for WordPress */
define('DB_NAME', 'database_name_here');

/** MySQL database username */
define('DB_USER', 'username_here');

/** MySQL database password */
define('DB_PASSWORD', 'password_here');

/** MySQL hostname */
define('DB_HOST', 'localhost');

/** Database Charset to use in creating database tables. */
define('DB_CHARSET', 'utf8');

/** The Database Collate type. Don't change this if in doubt. */
define('DB_COLLATE', '');

/**#@+
```

When you are finished, click ***File*** and ***Save As***, and name the file wp-config.php. Upload this file to the same location on the server as all of the other WordPress files, and try running the script again.

If you still cannot complete the installation, the WordPress.org forums are well-known for being extremely supportive and helpful. Consider asking a question on the site. Provide detailed information, including the name of your host, the stage at which you are stuck, and error codes, if any.[62]

62 http://wordpress.org/support/

Coding

If you are feeling particularly brave, you might find yourself delving into the code of your website. I will be frank, this can be dangerous in terms of damaging your site. Mess with the wrong line and suddenly you have errors, or even a site that will not work. Also, generally, editing a theme on WordPress requires knowledge of Cascading Style Sheets, known as CSS. This is not something with which the average person will be familiar.

I do not recommend that most users edit the code in WordPress, with one exception, which I will specifically walk you through in this appendix: changing the footer.

Where to Access the Theme's Code in WordPress

Accessing the code for a theme begins by clicking **Appearance** on your Dashboard. Next click on **Editor**. You will see a series of files on the right of the Dashboard. Click on the file you want to edit (see Figure C.1).

Figure C.1 Editing a Theme's Code

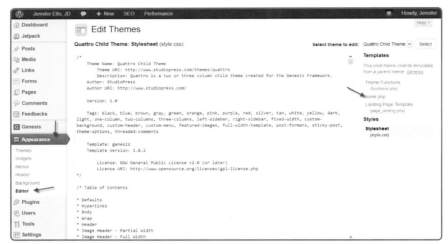

Creating a Child Theme

The first step in changing code in WordPress is to create something called a **child theme**. Then you make your coding changes in the child instead of the parent. The reason for this is twofold: First, if you need to upgrade the theme in the future (and in many cases you will), the child version will keep the changes you made. Second, if you make a mistake in the coding you can easily undo any damage by restoring the parent. This is because any coding changes will be made to the child and not to the parent.

Here is the process:

1. Open the text editor on your computer, such as Windows Notepad.
2. Create a file called **style.css**.

3. The theme will begin with language similar to what is shown in Figure C.2. The language you use will vary based on the theme with which you are working.

Figure C.2 Sample Code for Editing the Child Theme

```
/*
Theme Name:    Twenty Twelve Child
Theme URI:     http://example.com/
Description:   Child theme for the Twenty Twelve theme
Author:        Your name here
Author URI:    http://example.com/about/
Template:      twentytwelve
Version:       0.1.0
*/
```

4. You will also want to have the child theme work with the original theme, so you will need to use language similar to what is shown in Figure C.3; again, the language you use will depend on the theme with which you are working. Enter the language in the style.css page you have been creating.

Figure C.3 Code for Child Theme to Work with Parent Theme

```
@import url("../twentytwelve/style.css");
```

5. Now that you have completed the style.css page, you need to upload it to the same server as the rest of your site. The first step is to set up and use an FTP program[63] to connect to your web server.

6. Navigate to your WordPress theme directory via FTP.

7. Find the *wp-content* folder and then move into the *themes* folder.

8. Add a new folder with the same name as the theme, but with -*child* added to it. So if you are using the theme twentytwelve, you will name the folder twentytwelve-child.

---

63 FTP stands for File Transfer Protocol. An FTP program is used to transfer files from one location to another. Some good FTP programs include FileZilla and CuteFTP.

9. Upload your style.css file to the correct folder.

10. Return to the WordPress Dashboard.

11. Click on *Appearance*.

12. Click on *Themes*.

13. Locate your child theme.

14. Click *Activate*.

Now you are working from within the child theme instead of the parent theme. If you make a mistake, you can always delete what you wrote or even restore the parent as the active theme.[64]

Changing the Footer through Coding—without Creating a Child Theme

I think many people will find creating a child theme intimidating, so I want to provide an alternative for one area where you might want to change the theme: the footer. On many themes, you will need to change the footer on your own if you want to get rid of the Powered by Word-Press link and use your own footer.

In some themes, you will find an option for a footer, enabling you to easily put your disclaimer and copyright at the bottom of the site. Genesis users can install the plugin Genesis Simple Edits to handle this.[65] However, it is also not very difficult to edit one small part of the code in your site if your theme does not give you any footer options.

Again, please be very cautious in how you edit the code in your theme. You can easily destroy the functionality of part or all of your site if you are not careful.

---

64 For more details on working with child themes, see the WordPress.org Child Themes page at http://codex. wordpress.org/Child_Themes.

65 See Lesson 7 for more information about working with plugins.

The theme I am showing you how to edit here is the default WordPress theme, called Twenty Twelve.

1. Hover over ***Appearance*** and click on ***Editor*** as in Figure C.1.

2. Click on ***Footer.php***.

3. Click in the box where you see the code, and press **CTRL+A** on your keyboard. This will select the entire contents of the box.

4. Right-click with your mouse and click ***Copy***.

5. Open a text editor on your computer and paste this code into it. Save the file and keep it safe. You are creating this backup in case you make a mistake.

6. Return to WordPress.

7. Find the footer code (the highlighted text in Figure C.4) and delete it. This will remove the current footer referring to WordPress.[66]

---

66 WordPress's copyright allows for removal of the WordPress footer, as does the theme I am editing here. Check the copyright on any theme you use to determine if you are allowed to remove the footer.

Figure C.4 Deleting a WordPress Theme Footer

8. In place of the code you removed, put whatever content you want for your copyright and disclaimer. I recommend you link to your disclaimer page here. The code will look something like what is shown in Figure C.5.

9. Once you are done, click ***Update File***.

Figure C.5 Customized Footer Code

```
?>
        </div><!-- #main .wrapper -->
        <footer id="colophon" role="contentinfo">
            <div class="site-info">

<center> Nothing on this site is legal advice. Reading this site does not form an attorney/client
relationship between you and Jennifer Ellis, Esq. <br> Review the <a href="http://www.jlellis.net
/blog/contact/">full disclaimer</a> for more information. Copyright, Jennifer Ellis, JD. </center>



            </div><!-- .site-info -->
        </footer><!-- #colophon -->
</div><!-- #page -->
```

The code that reads <a href= is the link that sends people to my full disclaimer page. I used <center> to tell the code to center the line and </center> to tell it to stop centering. Using <br> creates a space, which helps me even out how the line appears. For more information on writing basic HTML code, I recommend w3schools, which contains excellent and simple lessons.[67]

The code I wrote in Figure C.5 appears on the bottom of my site as shown in Figure C.6.

Figure C.6 Customized Footer on Site

Nothing on this site is legal advice. Reading this site does not form an attorney/client relationship between you and Jennifer Ellis, Esq. Review the full disclaimer for more information. Copyright, Jennifer Ellis, JD.

If something goes wrong, take the code you saved in step 5 and paste it back in, replacing the code you damaged. Then try again. Make sure you always keep a clean copy of any text you will change. Also, once you are happy with your final code, keep a copy of that too. In the future, if you need to install an upgrade, you might lose your changes, and you will want to be able to paste them back in. If you prefer to avoid having to redo this if you upgrade your site in the future, use a child theme to make the change instead.

---

67 http://www.w3schools.com

Index

Entries marked *n* indicate that the reference is in a footnote. If there are multiple footnotes on a page the number after the *n* indicates which footnote is referenced.

H

hackers
  Admin username hacking, 20–21
  outdated plugins and, 64
  password breaking, 22
  WordPress targeting, 121–122
headers, 36
  creating, 42–45
  customizing, 42
headings, 105–106
  H1, H2, and H3 headings,
    105–106
  Paragraph, 105
home page, 101
  settings for, 27
honesty of communications, 116
HostGator, 6–7, 127
  as domain registrar, 16
  hosting fees, 9
hosting services. *See* web hosts
HTML, 141–147. *See also* coding
  for links within site, 71–73
Hummingbird search algorithm,
  104–105

I

images. *See also* media
  adding to site, 80–86
  alt text, 82, 84, 111

borders, 86
captions, 82, 84
copyrights, honoring, 82–83
linking, 80, 85–86
resizing, 84
SEO considerations, 111
settings, changing, 85–86
Smush.it plugin for, 84n
spacing around, 86
titles, 82
indexing of web sites, 101n
information display settings, 26–27
Insert Media page, 80–81
installation
  config file, 138–140
  with cPanel, 131n58
  database, creating, 130–133
  Famous 5-Minute Install, 130n
  Linux server for, 7
  manual, 129–140
  one-click installation, 2, 6,
    19–20, 126–127
  software, downloading, 133–140
  WordPress requirements, 7–8
installation script, running, 136–138
Install Themes tab, 34–35
  uploading themes, 37–38
interactive widgets box, 71
Internet Archive Wayback Machine,
  14
IP addresses, 17n18

R

SELECTED BOOKS FROM THE LAW PRACTICE DIVISION

The Lawyer's Guide to Microsoft Outlook 2013
By Dennis Kennedy and Allison C. Shields

Product Code: 5110752 • LP Price: $41.95 • Regular Price: $69.95

Take control of your e-mail, calendar, to-do list, and more with *The Lawyer's Guide to Microsoft® Outlook 2013*. This essential guide summarizes the most important new features in the newest version of Microsoft® Outlook and provides practical tips that will promote organization and productivity in your law practice. Written specifically for lawyers by a twenty-year veteran of law office technology and ABA member, this book will help you:

- Clean up your inbox and organize e-mail messages
- Manage appointments and meetings with your calendar
- Improve efficiency with the Outlook task list
- Track phone calls and time with the journal
- Search for e-mails and attachments
- Access Outlook from web and mobile devices
- Archive materials from old cases
- Troubleshoot when things go wrong
- Avoid Outlook mistakes commonly made by lawyers
- Save time with keyboard shortcuts
- And much more!

Blogging in One Hour for Lawyers
By Ernie Svenson

Product Code: 5110744 • LP Price: $24.95 • Regular Price: $39.95

Until a few years ago, only the largest firms could afford to engage an audience of millions. Now, lawyers in any size firm can reach a global audience at little to no cost—all because of blogs. An effective blog can help you promote your practice, become more "findable" online, and take charge of how you are perceived by clients, journalists and anyone who uses the Internet. Blogging in One Hour for Lawyers will show you how to create, maintain, and improve a legal blog—and gain new business opportunities along the way. In just one hour, you will learn to:

- Set up a blog quickly and easily
- Write blog posts that will attract clients
- Choose from various hosting options like Blogger, TypePad, and WordPress
- Make your blog friendly to search engines, increasing your ranking
- Tweak the design of your blog by adding customized banners and colors
- Easily send notice of your blog posts to Facebook and Twitter
- Monitor your blog's traffic with Google Analytics and other tools
- Avoid ethics problems that may result from having a legal blog

The Electronic Evidence and Discovery Handbook: Forms, Checklists, and Guidelines
By Sharon D. Nelson, Bruce A. Olson, and John W. Simek

Product Code: 5110569 • LP Price: $99.95 • Regular Price: $129.95

The use of electronic evidence has increased dramatically over the past few years, but many lawyers still struggle with the complexities of electronic discovery. This substantial book provides lawyers with the templates they need to frame their discovery requests and provides helpful advice on what they can subpoena. In addition to the ready-made forms, the authors also supply explanations to bring you up to speed on the electronic discovery field. The accompanying CD-ROM features over 70 forms, including, Motions for Protective Orders, Preservation and Spoliation Documents, Motions to Compel, Electronic Evidence Protocol Agreements, Requests for Production, Internet Services Agreements, and more. Also included is a full electronic evidence case digest with over 300 cases detailed!

Facebook® in One Hour for Lawyers
By Dennis Kennedy and Allison C. Shields

Product Code: 5110745 • LP Price: $24.95 • Regular Price: $39.95

With a few simple steps, lawyers can use Facebook® to market their services, grow their practices, and expand their legal network—all by using the same methods they already use to communicate with friends and family. *Facebook® in One Hour for Lawyers* will show any attorney—from Facebook® novices to advanced users—how to use this powerful tool for both professional and personal purposes.

Android Apps in One Hour for Lawyers
By Daniel J. Siegel

Product Code: 5110754 • LP Price: $19.95 • Regular Price: $34.95

Lawyers are already using Android devices to make phone calls, check e-mail, and send text messages. After the addition of several key apps, Android smartphones or tablets can also help run a law practice. From the more than 800,000 apps currently available, Android Apps in One Hour for Lawyers highlights the "best of the best" apps that will allow you to practice law from your mobile device. In just one hour, this book will describe how to buy, install, and update Android apps, and help you:

- Store documents and files in the cloud
- Use security apps to safeguard client data on your phone
- Be organized and productive with apps for to-do lists, calendar, and contacts
- Communicate effectively with calling, text, and e-mail apps
- Create, edit, and organize your documents
- Learn on the go with news, reading, and reference apps
- Download utilities to keep your device running smoothly
- Hit the road with apps for travel
- Have fun with games and social media apps

Virtual Law Practice:
How to Deliver Legal Services Online
By Stephanie L. Kimbro

Product Code: 5110707 • **LP Price:** $47.95 • **Regular Price:** $79.95

The legal market has recently experienced a dramatic shift as lawyers seek out alternative methods of practicing law and providing more affordable legal services. Virtual law practice is revolutionizing the way the public receives legal services and how legal professionals work with clients. If you are interested in this form of practicing law, *Virtual Law Practice* will help you:

- Responsibly deliver legal services online to your clients
- Successfully set up and operate a virtual law office
- Establish a virtual law practice online through a secure, client-specific portal
- Manage and market your virtual law practice
- Understand state ethics and advisory opinions
- Find more flexibility and work/life balance in the legal profession

Social Media for Lawyers: The Next Frontier
By Carolyn Elefant and Nicole Black

Product Code: 5110710 • **LP Price:** $47.95 • **Regular Price:** $79.95

The world of legal marketing has changed with the rise of social media sites such as Linkedin, Twitter, and Facebook. Law firms are seeking their companies attention with tweets, videos, blog posts, pictures, and online content. Social media is fast and delivers news at record pace. This book provides you with a practical, goal-centric approach to using social media in your law practice that will enable you to identify social media platforms and tools that fit your practice and implement them easily, efficiently, and ethically.

iPad Apps in One Hour for Lawyers
By Tom Mighell

Product Code: 5110739 • **LP Price:** $19.95 • **Regular Price:** $34.95

At last count, there were more than 80,000 apps available for the iPad. Finding the best apps often can be an overwhelming, confusing, and frustrating process. iPad Apps in One Hour for Lawyers provides the "best of the best" apps that are essential for any law practice. In just one hour, you will learn about the apps most worthy of your time and attention. This book will describe how to buy, install, and update iPad apps, and help you:

- Find apps to get organized and improve your productivity
- Create, manage, and store documents on your iPad
- Choose the best apps for your law office, including litigation and billing apps
- Find the best news, reading, and reference apps
- Take your iPad on the road with apps for travelers
- Maximize your social networking power
- Have some fun with game and entertainment apps during your relaxation time

Twitter in One Hour for Lawyers
By Jared Correia

Product Code: 5110746 • **LP Price:** $24.95 • **Regular Price:** $39.95

More lawyers than ever before are using Twitter to network with colleagues, attract clients, market their law firms, and even read the news. But to the uninitiated, Twitter's short messages, or tweets, can seem like they are written in a foreign language. Twitter in One Hour for Lawyers will demystify one of the most important social-media platforms of our time and teach you to tweet like an expert. In just one hour, you will learn to:

- Create a Twitter account and set up your profile
- Read tweets and understand Twitter jargon
- Write tweets—and send them at the appropriate time
- Gain an audience—follow and be followed
- Engage with other Twitters users
- Integrate Twitter into your firm's marketing plan
- Cross-post your tweets with other social media platforms like Facebook and LinkedIn
- Understand the relevant ethics, privacy, and security concerns
- Get the greatest possible return on your Twitter investment
- And much more!

The Lawyer's Essential Guide to Writing
By Marie Buckley

Product Code: 5110726 • **LP Price:** $47.95 • **Regular Price:** $79.95

This is a readable, concrete guide to contemporary legal writing. Based on Marie Buckley's years of experience coaching lawyers, this book provides a systematic approach to all forms of written communication, from memoranda and briefs to e-mail and blogs. The book sets forth three principles for powerful writing and shows how to apply those principles to develop a clean and confident style.

iPad in One Hour for Lawyers, Second Edition
By Tom Mighell

Product Code: 5110747 • **LP Price:** $24.95 • **Regular Price:** $39.95

Whether you are a new or a more advanced iPad user, *iPad in One Hour for Lawyers* takes a great deal of the mystery and confusion out of using your iPad. Ideal for lawyers who want to get up to speed swiftly, this book presents the essentials so you don't get bogged down in technical jargon and extraneous features and apps. In just six, short lessons, you'll learn how to:

- Quickly Navigate and Use the iPad User Interface
- Set Up Mail, Calendar, and Contacts
- Create and Use Folders to Multitask and Manage Apps
- Add Files to Your iPad, and Sync Them
- View and Manage Pleadings, Case Law, Contracts, and other Legal Documents
- Use Your iPad to Take Notes and Create Documents
- Use Legal-Specific Apps at Trial or in Doing Research

30-DAY RISK-FREE ORDER FORM

ABA LAW PRACTICE DIVISION
The Business of Practicing Law

Please print or type. To ship UPS, we must have your street address. If you list a P.O. Box, we will ship by U.S. Mail.

Name

Member ID

Firm/Organization

Street Address

City/State/Zip

Area Code/Phone (In case we have a question about your order)

E-mail

Method of Payment:
☐ Check enclosed, payable to American Bar Association
☐ MasterCard   ☐ Visa   ☐ American Express

Card Number   Expiration Date

Signature Required

MAIL THIS FORM TO:
American Bar Association, Publication Orders
P.O. Box 10892, Chicago, IL 60610

ORDER BY PHONE:
24 hours a day, 7 days a week:
Call 1-800-285-2221 to place a credit card order. We accept Visa, MasterCard, and American Express.

EMAIL ORDERS: orders@americanbar.org
FAX ORDERS: 1-312-988-5568

VISIT OUR WEB SITE: www.ShopABA.org
Allow 7-10 days for regular UPS delivery. Need it sooner? Ask about our overnight delivery options. Call the ABA Service Center at 1-800-285-2221 for more information.

GUARANTEE:
If–for any reason–you are not satisfied with your purchase, you may return it within 30 days of receipt for a refund of the price of the book(s). No questions asked.

Thank You For Your Order.

Join the ABA Law Practice Division today and receive a substantial discount on Division publications!

Product Code:	Description:	Quantity:	Price:	Total Price:
				$
				$
				$
				$
				$

**Shipping/Handling:		***Tax:**		
$0.00 to $9.99	add $0.00	IL residents add 9.25%	**Subtotal:**	$
$10.00 to $49.99	add $6.95	DC residents add 6%	***Tax:**	$
$50.00 to $99.99	add $8.95		****Shipping/Handling:**	$
$100.00 to $199.99	add $10.95	Yes, I am an ABA member and would like to join the Law Practice Division today! (Add $50.00)		$
$200.00 to $499.99	add $13.95		**Total:**	$